Dedicated to the memory
of those given refuge
at the
Guildford Union Workhouse
and the
Vagrants' Casual Ward

"The Spike"

by

Helen Chapman Davies

By the same author:

The Story of Onslow Village. A New and Greater Guildford. 1999.

Diseases, Privies and Rubbish. With Highlights from Guildford's Past.
The archaeology and history of public health. 2002.

Acknowledgements

I would like to express my sincere thanks to the staff of the Surrey History Service and Guildford Museum to whom I am deeply indebted for all their help in researching the information for this book and for allowing me to reproduce documentary and photographic material. I am extremely grateful to Anne Bowey for all her help with the documentary research and to David Rose, Peter and Val Harfleet, John Adams and Victor Beard for allowing me to reproduce photographic material. Thanks are due to members of the Guildford Archaeology and Local History Group for their help in recording the Vagrants' Casual Ward. I am also greatly indebted to Dr Brian Ward for reading the manuscript and for his invaluable advice.

Published by
Guildford Museum
Quarry Street
Guildford
Surrey GU1 3SX

Copyright © Guildford Museum, 2004
All rights reserved. No part of this publication may be reproduced, stored in a retrieval system, or transmitted in any form or by any means electrical, mechanical, photocopied, recorded or otherwise, without the prior permission of Guildford Museum.

Typeset, Printed & Bound in the UK
by
Guildford Borough Council
Printing Department

ISBN 0-9543753-1-9

Contents

Acknowledgements	iii
Contents	vii
Illustrations	ix
Early Provision for the Destitute	1
Poor Relief, Vagrancy and the Origins of the Workshouse	5
The Poor Law Amendment Act of 1834 and the Victorian Workhouse	11
The Guildford Union Workhouse	17
The Vagrants' Casual Ward "The Spike"	27
From Union Workshouse to St. Luke's Hospital	49

Appendices

Appendix 1	Guildford Union. Extract from the Quarterly Abstract for the Quarter ending 24th September, 1836	54
Appendix 2	Guildford Union. Extract from the Quarterly Abstract for the Quarter ending 24th March 1838	55
Appendix 3	Guildford Union. Extract from the Quarterly Abstract for the Quarter ending 21st March 1840	56
Appendix 4	Guildford Union. Items of Expenditure as detailed on 24th April 1840	57
Appendix 5	Abstract of the Census of the Population of the Guildford District of the Guildford Union, taken 7th June 1841	58
Appendix 6	Guildford Union. Extract from the Quarterly Abstract for the Quarter ending 21st September 1844	59
Appendix 7	Items of Expenditure as detailed on 23rd October 1844	60

Appendices 1-7 reproduced by permission of Guildford Museum

Afterword 61

Sources 62

Bibliography of other useful suggested sources 64

Glossary of Terms 65

Illustrations

Fig.1 Map of the Guildford Poor Law Union.
(By permission of Guildford Museum).

Fig.2 Ordnance Survey map showing the Guildford Union Workhouse. (50" Sheet XXIV. 13, 21. Pub. 1871. Surveyed 1868. Reproduced by permission of Surrey History Service. Copyright of Surrey History Service).

Fig.3 Plan of Guildford Union Casual Ward for men, women and women with children. February 7th, 1905 by Edward L. Lunn, Architect, Guildford. (Item 5118/Box 78 plan 2852. Reproduced by permission of Surrey History Service. Copyright of Guildford Borough Council).

Fig.4 The Department for Culture, Media and Sport Listing of the Guildford Union Casual Ward, 16th November 1999.
(Reproduced from author's own copy).

Plate 1 Illustration of the Guildford Union Workhouse.
(Document PX/72/610. Reproduced by permission of Surrey History Service. Copyright of Surrey History Service).

Plate 2 The Guildford Union Casual Ward.
(Photograph: Author).

Plate 3 Salt-glazed bricks in the corridor of the men's casual ward.
(Photograph reproduced by permission of David Rose).

Plate 4 The remaining in situ iron grills of the stone-breaking work cells, men's casual ward.
(Photograph: Author).

Plate 5 The outside waiting room. Guildford Union Casual Ward.
(Photograph: Author)

Plate 6 Entrance to accommodation for Tramp Master and Mistress. Guildford Union Casual Ward.
(Photograph: Author).

Plate 7 Entrance to Guildford Union Casual Ward from Warren Road. The corner of the roof of the outside waiting room can be seen bottom right.
(Photograph by permission of Peter and Val Harfleet).

Plate 8 The corridor in the men's casual ward showing cells on either side.
(Photograph by permission of David Rose).

Plate 9 Wooden door between sleeping and work cell in men's casual ward.
(Photograph by permission of Victor Beard).

Plate 10 Interior of sleeping cell leading into stone-breaking cell, men's casual ward.
(Photograph by permission of Victor Beard).

Plate 11 Interior of stone-breaking work cell showing iron grill.
(Photograph by permission of Peter and Val Harfleet).

Plate 12 Door to sleeping cell in men's casual ward showing spyhole, site of lock (now missing) and bolt at bottom of door.
(Photograph by permission of Peter and Val Harfleet).

Plate 13 Inside of door in men's casual ward sleeping cell showing spyhole.
(Photograph by permission of David Rose).

Plate 14 Graffiti on the inside of one of the cell doors, men's casual ward.
(Photograph by permission of David Rose).

Plate 15 A picture taken in April 1963 showing the lantern lights in situ, above the casual ward.
(Photograph by permission of John Adams).

Plate 16 A picture taken in 1962 showing tramps queuing outside the casual ward.
(Photograph by permission of John Adams).

Plate 17 The door that led into the men's casual ward.
(Photograph: Author 1999).

Plate 18   Warren Road, Guildford. The casual ward is on the right. Opposite are stone walls in which tramps hid money, etc.
(Photograph: Author).

Plate 19   The women's casual ward at the west end of the building.
(Photograph: Author 1999).

Plate 20   A picture taken later in 1962 of the entrance to the casual ward in Warren Road, now closed.
(Photograph by permission of John Adams).

Plate 21   The infirmary and part of the workhouse in use as Guildford Military Hospital during the First World War, showing the workhouse entrance. (Postcard reference number 67923 from Folio 9A Guildford Photograph Album Number 4. Page 17. Guildford Military War Hospital. Reproduced by permission of Surrey History Service. Copyright of Surrey History Service).

Plate 22   The infirmary and part of the workhouse in use as Guildford Military Hospital during the First World War, showing the workhouse entrance. (Postcard reference number 67924 from Folio 9A Guildford Photograph Album Number 4. Page 17. Guildford Military War Hospital. Reproduced by permission of Surrey History Service. Copyright of Surrey History Service).

Plate 23   A picture taken in 1999 showing the west end of the casual ward on the left. The building on the right was part of St Luke's Hospital, since demolished. (Photograph: Author).

Chapter I

Early provision for the destitute

The provision of shelter for orphans, the destitute, infirm, sick, mentally ill and the elderly is coupled with the history of medical hospitals and covers a period of time from about the 3rd century BC to the present day. The first recorded institution was an isolation hospital in Italy set up on an island in the river Tiber following an outbreak of plague in Rome in 293 BC, which was later renamed St Bartholomew's. Hospitals were provided as charitable institutions endowed by the wealthy both to provide sanctuary for the destitute and the sick and as a means of keeping such undesirables off the streets and out of sight. These institutions did not, however, provide any form of medical care. The church and the monastic orders saw the provision of shelter and care for the sick and destitute as an obligation and an infirmarium or sick ward was a part of the monastic institution. Other institutions originated independently of monastic foundation and the oldest in Western Europe was the Hotel Dieu in Paris, founded by the Bishop of Paris in 600 AD. The reign of Charlemagne (768-814 AD) saw the establishment of hospitals of various kinds throughout his kingdom and this influence seems to have spread to Britain. A Saxon hospital is recorded at St Albans in 794 AD and St Peter's Hospital in York was founded by Athelstan in 937. As well as building castles and cathedrals, the Normans also established hospitals to provide shelter for the destitute, for the physically and mentally sick and especially for lepers. Two such establishments, run by the Augustinian order, were St Bartholomew's in London, founded shortly after 1123 and St Thomas's, whose original infirmary is believed to be under or very close to Southwark Cathedral.

Despite the dissolution of the monasteries and religious foundations by Henry VIII, some of these former monastic buildings continued in use as parochial or corporate institutions, offering shelter to the destitute and the sick. There was no medical provision for the sick, however, in the form of attempted cures or treatment. The endowment of almshouses by the wealthy to provide shelter for 'deserving' poor families also continued. Throughout the seventeenth and eighteenth centuries, various Acts of Parliament were passed, including a general Act in 1723 empowering parishes to join together into small 'unions' for the purpose of building 'working houses' to provide employment for paupers and hospitals to give shelter to the sick and infirm. During the nineteenth century, voluntary hospitals were set up in most major cities, financed by fees and charitable subscriptions, which gave free in-patient and out-patient care to the poor among the local population. In some areas care was given to all those in need, while in other areas care was available to those able to produce a letter from a charitable subscriber vouching for their good character and financial circumstances. However, in 1851 it was reported that there were fewer than eight thousand beds in public hospitals in England and Wales and that by 1871 there were still only some twenty thousand beds. According to a survey of 1894-5, between thirty and forty percent of all persons over the age of sixty-five were paupers, but the stigma of the workhouse was such that the destitute and the sick would accept any privation rather than be obliged to become an inmate. It was ironic that whilst the intention of the Victorian workhouse was to act as a deterrent to the able-bodied poor, it was also intended as a refuge for the elderly, the sick and the infirm, and in fact great improvements had been made in the standards of care in workhouse infirmaries and hospitals. An innovation of the Victorian period was the introduction for those who could afford it, of financial provision against personal sickness. By 1900, it was estimated that some four million workers were covered by some form of contributory sickness insurance offered by friendly societies, trade unions and the newly developing industrial assurance companies. Various charitable and commercial establishments also offered help to the needy sick including medical missions, provident dispensaries, as well as schemes to raise money for local hospitals. A wide variety of pharmacists and homeopaths came into being, one of whom was Jesse Boot, the son of a travelling herbalist and healer, who became the founder of the nation's largest chain of retail chemist shops.

A major problem in hospital care was nursing. Nurses were drawn mainly from elderly, often illiterate ex-domestic servants who were totally untrained, poorly paid and given the worst possible living conditions. Ward sisters and matrons were drawn from a higher social class but were not involved with the work of the nursing staff. In the workhouse infirmaries, virtually the entire nursing staff was drawn from elderly able-bodied inmates who were unpaid and untaught and often rewarded with a gin ration for laying out the dead and other unpleasant duties. The Nightingale School, which opened in June 1860 in St. Thomas's Hospital, was founded by Florence Nightingale as "An institution for the training, assistance and protection of nurses and hospital attendants". This reinforced a movement that was taking place for the reform of the Poor Law infirmaries. In the opinion of a select committee on medical relief reporting in 1864, the poor were well cared for. However, a year later an investigation by the medical journal *The Lancet* exposed the state of neglect in many workhouse infirmaries. Subsequently, Florence Nightingale made representations to the president of the Poor Law Board. Working with the Poor Law Inspector for the Metropolitan District, a plan was drawn up "To insist on the great principles of separating the sick, insane, incurable and above all, children from the usual population of the metropolis ... and to provide for a 'general hospital rate' to be levied over the whole Metropolitan area". An Act of 1867 made provision for Poor Law infirmaries, with a resident medical superintendent, to be completely separate from the workhouse and from the jurisdiction of the workhouse master. Although Florence Nightingale had demanded more legislation, this was a beginning and the Act of 1867 dominated subsequent legislation until the transfer of responsibility to local authorities in 1929.

Until the end of the 19th century, hospitals had been provided for the shelter or, as Miss Nightingale put it, a "storehouse for the sick", while those who could afford it were treated at home. At the beginning of the twentieth the wealthier classes were beginning to go into hospital for serious treatment for the first time in history and the role of hospitals changed as a result. This might have posed the risk that some hospitals, rather than fulfilling their statutory duties to the poor, might be 'taken over' as institutions for the rich. Such a reversal had happened to the Public Schools, which had been founded to educate the children of the poor whilst those who could afford it educated their children at home. However, many of the Poor Law workhouse infirmaries were transformed into public hospitals and new public hospitals were built, while the National Health Service Act that came into force on 5th July 1948 provided a controlling body for hospitals.

Sources:

Harris, Jose.	*Private Lives Public Spirit. A Social History of Britain 1870-1914.* 1993. Oxford University Press.
Harrison, J.F.C.	*Late Victorian Britain 1875-1901.* 1990. Fontana Press.
Ives, A.G.L.	*British Hospitals.* MCMXLVIII. Collins, London.
Johnson, Paul.	*A Place in History.* 1974. Weidenfeld & Nicholson.

Chapter 2

Poor relief, vagrancy and the origins of the workhouse

Poverty and vagrancy were fluctuating national problems which increased during periods of work shortages brought about by climatic and economic circumstances. At such times men and indeed whole families, took to the road in search of employment. Whilst outbreaks of diseases, such as the plague, caused a great number of deaths, this in turn brought about a shortage in the workforce and as a result, labourers and workmen were in great demand. Following the ravages of the Black Death, which reached England in 1348, an Act forbade the provision of relief to able-bodied beggars in order to oblige them to seek employment. Restrictions were put on the movement of vagrants and unemployed labourers under a further Act of 1388 which made the hundred responsible for relieving its destitute. Vagrants and beggars were further subjected to an Act of 1494 requiring them to find employment or risk punishment in the stocks, although the infirm were permitted to beg within their own hundred.

Vagrancy became a severe problem during the 16th century. There was a rising population, monetary inflation, while many landowners turned arable land over to pasture for sheep ranching, depriving tenant farmers and agricultural workers of their livelihood. With the loss of ecclesiastical sources of help for the destitute and the sick following the dissolution of the monasteries and suppression of religious institutions by Henry VIII between 1536 and 1539, there was often no alternative but to take to the road in search of work or to beg for alms.

The extent of vagrancy was seen as a threat to the social and economic stability of the nation and so Parliament took steps to place increasing responsibility for the poor on the parish. An Act of 1536 ordered churchwardens to collect voluntary sums of money for poor relief and to find work for the able-bodied poor, although this proved difficult to apply. A Statute of 1547 called for the branding of vagrants and beggars although relief was to be provided for the infirm poor and dwellings provided for their shelter. An instruction of 1572 required Justices to compile a register of the destitute and sick and to tax householders accordingly to provide a means of poor relief. Further legislation of 1598 called for parish churchwardens and appointed overseers to find work for children and paupers and to provide relief for the infirm. This was paid for by levying a tax on landowners.

These various pieces of legislation, introduced in an attempt to relieve the poor and to deal with vagrancy, culminated in what became known as the Elizabethan Poor Laws or the Act of Elizabeth of 1601. Referred to subsequently as The Old Poor Law, the Act established a system of parish responsibility for those unable to support themselves, particularly widows, orphans, the elderly, the sick and unmarried mothers. Poor relief was applied in two forms. 'Outdoor relief' was paid as a weekly sum of money or 'dole', or in the form of food or fuel, according to need. 'Indoor relief' relied on providing employment in one form or another in a purpose-built 'working house' or manufactory. A poor rate was levied on owners and occupiers of land and property who were assessed according the size of their holding. The rate was collected by parish officers, or overseers of the poor, who served in a voluntary capacity and distributed relief according to need. Under the system the elderly and the sick were to be maintained while work was to be provided for the able-bodied poor in purpose-built workhouses or manufactures.

An Act of 1623 encouraged the establishment of 'hospitals' and 'working houses' for the poor. In 1630 Charles I set up a body known as the Commissioners for the Poor to investigate the extent to which the poor laws were being administered. By about 1640 the poor rate was being used by many urban parishes to provide 'hospitals' as shelter for children and the elderly and 'working houses' in which to employ the able-bodied or to assist local employers to take them. These working houses were intended as places of work and not for the shelter of the poor. The workhouses that were set up in the 17th century were more like workshops or small factories, generally for textile manufacture, and were mostly set up in towns where other sources of work for the poor were not available.

The parish was also required to punish those who refused the work they were offered. An Act of 1576 called for every city and town to provide a 'house of correction' in which to detain and punish those who refused to work. As a result, buildings used as hospitals or working houses often included or were situated close to a 'house of correction' or 'bridewell', which took its name from Bridewell in London, an institution that became the model for many houses of correction in England. It was also laid down that every county should have one or more houses of correction where materials and implements should be provided to set the idle to work. However the Act does not appear to have been implemented in Guildford or indeed in Surrey. The Act's instructions were repeated in 1598 and in 1610 a further Act demanded the instructions were applied and if not, all Justices were to be fined. The first house of correction in Guildford was in the

High Street. At some time before 1660, buildings fronting the High Street from The Shambles to the corner of Quarry Street were bought by the Surrey Justices for the purpose. A new house of correction was built in 1767 in grounds at the back of the High Street buildings to replace this now dilapidated building. A third replacement house of correction was built on South Hill in 1820 which closed in around 1852.

An early example of a workhouse in Guildford was the Manufactory set up by Archbishop George Abbot in a building to the west of the garden of his hospital at the top of North Street, designed to house up to 50 paupers. This was completed in 1630 and founded as a charity known as the Manufacturing Endowment which Archbishop Abbot hoped would help to restore prosperity to the cloth industry in Guildford and employ the pauper inmates. To begin with, out-of-work cloth workers were employed to produce linen. This failed because there was little demand for the product so a change was made to woollen cloth production. However, by 1655 the venture had failed, the workhouse was divided into four cottages and the annual sum from the Endowment was distributed among needy inhabitants of the cottages. At some time between 1660 and 1673 the three Guildford parishes of St Mary, St Nicholas and Holy Trinity united to build a workhouse which incorporated the Manufactory, while the Manufactory itself became the workhouse infirmary. A medical officer associated with Guildford's early workhouse was William Newland, surgeon and doctor. He was appointed in 1779 to inspect and order the provisions and other necessities for the workhouse maintained by St Mary's Church. (This workhouse is assumed to be the one built by the 'union' of parishes of St Mary, St Nicholas and Holy Trinity incorporating Archbishop Abbot's Manufactory). Following the Poor Law Amendment Act of 1834, this workhouse was sold by the Board of Guardians and was divided into cottages. In 1855 the Endowment monies were combined with the charity monies of Guildford's Bluecoat School and the workhouse cottages were converted into a school endowed by the amalgamated monies. The school closed in 1933, the buildings were bought by the governors of Abbot's Hospital and leased to Clark's College. In 1891 the existing tower was built. By about 1862 the North Street end of the building had become the Crown Inn beer house which was sold by the school's trustees to the Corporation and demolished in 1907.

The Laws of Settlement of 1662 confirmed the local character of poor relief. Any stranger to a parish who had no prospect of work within forty days, or who did not rent a property to the value of ten pounds per annum, could be removed from the parish by the overseer. Any person employed in casual labour, for example during the harvest, had to obtain a certificate from his home parish guaranteeing to take him back when his work was complete.

Towards the end of the 17th century, there was a harsher attitude towards paupers, with distinction being made between the "deserving" and the "undeserving" poor.

Poor relief and charity were seen to be in opposition to the concept of hard work and thrift. Rather than recognise the causes of poverty in economic and social terms with low wages and trade depression, poverty was believed to be brought about by idleness and irresponsibility. Whilst no major changes were made to the original Act of 1601, minor pieces of legislation were passed in the form of amendments in an attempt to alleviate the problems of administering poor relief. In 1691, an Act was passed that required a register to be kept of parishioners in receipt of poor relief. The Settlement Act of 1697 allowed strangers to settle in a new parish if they were in possession of a certificate from their home parish stating it would take them back should they become in need of poor relief. The Act obliged paupers to wear a badge with a capital 'P' followed by a letter indicating the name of their parish. In their own parish, application for poor relief had to be made to the overseer of the poor or to the local magistrate.

Workhouses had been particularly difficult to establish and run on any sort of economic basis in small rural parishes and so larger administrative areas were proposed with up to six parishes combining into 'unions' to set up workhouses. Various proposals were made throughout the 17th and into the 18th centuries for setting the poor to work to ease the rising poor rates but little was achieved. In the early 18th century, a number of larger towns set up residential workhouses, some in former ecclesiastical buildings. Until 1723 a special Act of Parliament had to be obtained by any parish wishing to build a workhouse. The General Workhouse Act of 1723 empowered overseers, with the consent of the vestry, to build workhouses in single parishes and for several smaller parishes to join together as a 'union' to provide a workhouse. The intention of these workhouses was to put the poor to work. However, the measure led to a stringent workhouse test whereby anyone claiming poor relief who refused to accept employment in the workhouse, gave up the right to any relief at all. There was no segregation of the sexes or of children and the often appalling conditions caused much condemnation throughout the 18th and into the first four decades of the 19th centuries.

By 1776 there were reported to be over 2,000 workhouses in England, suggesting they were seen as an effective way of dealing with the poor. However, social attitudes to poverty began to change with some recognition of the plight of the poor and destitute. Gilbert's Act of Parliament of 1782 eased some of the harshness of the workhouse test and encouraged parishes to join together in 'unions' to build joint poorhouses or workhouses. Three such 'unions' or incorporations existed in the Guildford area: Godalming, Worplesdon and the joint parish of Send and Ripley. The poorhouse properties of Guildford's three parishes of St Mary, St Nicholas and Holy Trinity comprised two cottages in Millmead, four houses belonging to Holy Trinity and two houses belonging to St Mary. Some of the outlying parishes had their own poorhouses, for example Albury, Merrow, Ockham, Woking, Compton, East Clandon, Stoke, Shere and Wisley, all of which were sold in 1837 and 1838 to raise money to build union workhouses. Local inspectors were appointed to check on conditions in workhouses in their locality. Able-bodied paupers were to be found work outside the workhouse and orphaned children were boarded out. Paupers of good character were no longer obliged to wear the pauper badge.

Another means of poor relief was the 'roundsman' system. One measure under this system was to send unemployed labourers round the parish in search of work until someone was willing to take them on for a wage subsidised by the parish. Another measure was the imposition of a labour rate compelling each ratepayer to employ a certain number of labourers according to his poor-rate assessment, or to pay the parish a sum equal to their wages if he had no work. In 1795 the Laws of Settlement were made less harsh and in that same year the Speenhamland system was introduced. This legislation sought to regulate poor relief according to the price of bread and the size of a man's family and was widely adopted once authorised by Parliament. It was seen as a measure of poor relief to allow for the devastating effects on the agricultural workforce brought about by enclosure.

The mid-19th century again saw a rise in the numbers of destitute and vagrants brought about by a rapidly rising population, the growth of industrial towns with fluctuating employment and returning soldiers and militiamen following the end of the Napoleonic wars in 1815. At the census of 1801 the population was just under eleven million. The census of 1831 revealed that this figure had risen to sixteen and a half million. For example Manchester had a population of about 40,000 in 1770 rising to 187,000 by 1821. Poverty was further increased by a series of poor harvests from the mid 19th century which brought job losses in agricultural employment as high wheat prices plummeted and farming struggled to cope with a series of bad summers and winters. With the Irish potato famine at its worst in the 1840s and 1850s, large numbers of people migrated to England in search of work. The Highland Clearances of the 1840s combined with changes in agricultural practice in Scotland also brought a movement of Scots southwards into England looking for work.

There was a marked increase in the cost of poor relief, from some two million pounds in 1784 to about seven million pounds in 1832. As a result the system of poor relief was overhauled between 1832 and 1834, resulting in the Poor Law Amendment Act. The intention of the reformers had been to return to the spirit of the Elizabethan Poor Law whereby each parish was responsible for the maintenance of its paupers, particularly the elderly and the sick, with work provided for the able-bodied in workhouses set up for that purpose.

Sources:

Green, J.K.	*Sidelights on Guildford History III.* 1954. Reprinted edition by permission of the Surrey Times.
Morrison, Kathryn.	*The Workhouse. A Study of Poor Law Buildings in England.* 1999. English Heritage.
Noyes, Ann.	*Shere Poverty. From Parish Workhouse to Union Workhouse. 1996.* Twiga Books. Gomshall, Surrey.
Taylor, Brian.	*Abbot's Hospital, Guildford.* 1999. St Thomas's Trust, Guildford.
Thompson, Beryl.	*Life in the Workhouse, Booklet 3, Vagrants.* 1996. Ripon Museum Trust.
Wheeleker, Susannah & Eyles, Sarah.	*Poor Relief in Devon.* 1991. The Devonshire Association.

Chapter 3

The Poor Law Amendment Act of 1834 and the Victorian Workhouse

An Act for the Amendment and Better Administration of the laws relating to the Poor in England and Wales. 14th August 1834.

The Poor Law Amendment Act was contentious because the method adopted for dealing with the problem of the poor and destitute was deliberately harsh. The argument for the harshness was that people were poor because they were idle and that going into the workhouse should be seen as a last resort and a punishment for their poverty, not as a source of help. Another criticism was the bureaucracy involved in setting up the Act with its headquarters at Somerset House in London, supervised by three commissioners who controlled the work of twenty-two assistant commissioners who set up the new unions.

Under the conditions of the Act parishes were combined into Poor Law Unions. Each union was to consist of about twenty parishes and was to be administered by an elected board of guardians. By 1838 over 13,000 parishes had been incorporated into 573 unions. In financial terms, the Act was extremely successful. The poor rate in Surrey fell from 10s.9d (10 shillings and 9 pence) per head of population in 1834 to 6s.4d in 1837. Sussex had the highest rate at 18s.1d in 1834, which fell to 8s.7d in 1837.

It was intended that conditions in the workhouse were to be harsher than those of the poorest labourer and that all able-bodied persons who sought poor relief were to be put into the workhouse. However, this was not an appropriate remedy for short periods of industrial distress when out-relief was resorted to and charitable sources of help such as the soup kitchen were common. Indeed in the early 1860s it was calculated that philanthropic activity in London amounted to between five and a half million and seven million pounds annually. This figure was not far short of the total expenditure on the administration of the Poor Law throughout England and Wales.

Union workhouses were built at a distance of about twenty miles (32 km) apart. By 1883 a total of 554 new workhouses had been built. As a token gesture to civic pride many were designed with elegant facades, but the interior of the various model plans resembled prisons with their high walls enclosing gaunt buildings and segregated exercise yards. In common parlance the workhouse became known as the 'bastille', referring to the famous French prison, or 'the spike', referring to the spikes used in picking oakum, one of the tasks given to inmates, or simply 'the house'.

Because of the social stigma attached to them, workhouses were built centrally to the union so that paupers could reach them on foot but were located on the very periphery of towns. Men, women and children were segregated and separated again into groups of able-bodied, the aged and the infirm. On arrival new inmates were obliged to wash, have their hair cut in a rough standard manner and wear workhouse dress. Children attending school outside the workhouse were immediately recognised as workhouse inmates and their lives made even more miserable. Often workhouses had to be extended in size to take in greater numbers of paupers and to provide more hospital accommodation for the sick. Nevertheless charities continued to coexist with the Poor Law, while established almshouses continued in use and many new ones were built. Charitable aid was often greater in ancient towns with their smaller population than in the new and growing industrial towns and cities where there were greater numbers of poor.

The master of the workhouse was generally seen in the same terms as a jailer and candidates for the post were frequently former policemen or ex-army and navy non-commissioned officers. Salaries were low with no career prospects and until 1896 there were no pension rights. In 1880, the master of a workhouse holding between 500 and 600 inmates might earn £80 per year, while the governor of a prison for 900 prisoners could earn £600 per year. It was standard practice to appoint a married couple as master and mistress of the workhouse.

In 1842 the Poor Law Commissioners tried to insist that workhouse medical officers held a medical qualification. The work was poorly paid with no status and to begin with doctors were expected to provide their own drugs and medical supplies. It was the Medical Act of 1858 that laid the foundation for the professional status of doctors and medical staff began to play an increasingly important role as the sick and infirm came to represent the majority of workhouse inmates. To begin with, nursing requirements were carried out by female inmates who might be rewarded with gin for carrying out the more unpleasant tasks such as laying out the dead. Only the most basic qualifications were laid down, although Article 165 of the Consolidated Orders of 1847 did state that *'No person shall hold the office of Nurse who is not able to read directions upon medicines'*. It was after the 1860s that trained and paid nurses began to be employed.

The medical journal *The Lancet* began enquiries in the 1860s into the inadequacies of medical provision in workhouses. Following the Metropolitan Poor Act of 1867, Poor Law Unions began to establish infirmaries as separate buildings. By 1896 nearly 59,000 pauper patients were being treated in workhouse sick wards or separate infirmaries. The Diseases Prevention Act of 1883 removed the penalty of disenfranchisement from those receiving treatment in workhouse hospitals and expressly authorised the admission of non-paupers. When the Royal Commission on the Poor Law of 1905-1909 came into effect, some Poor Law hospitals were so good that the guardians could operate in effect a private payment system for medical treatment.

The Poor Law schoolteacher had a lower status than the workhouse medical officer. Between 1835 and 1908, about one third of all those receiving poor relief were children under the age of 16. It was felt that giving children an education might help to keep them from destitution and great advances were made in improving pauper education. These advances were particularly inspired by Dr James Kay (later Sir James Kay-Shuttleworth) who pioneered developments in both the curriculum and the training of teachers in Poor Law schools and these developments were extended to elementary schools. It became the intention to educate children outside the workhouse, either in Poor Law district schools or in the elementary schools. In 1913 the central authorities issued an order compelling the removal of children from the workhouse, either by placing them in separate boarding houses, by fostering them, or by putting orphans up for adoption.

The workhouse diet was meagre and of extremely poor quality and, together with the harsh living conditions, was used as a means of making the workhouse the last possible option for the destitute. The last meal of the day was often as early as 5pm and breakfast the next day at 8am. Dietaries were drawn up by the boards of guardians, the quantities of food rigidly standardised and accounted for. The staple diet consisted of bread, cheese, a thin oatmeal porridge, soup, potatoes and occasionally meat and bacon. Six model diets laid down by the Poor Law Board provided for between 137 and 182 ounces of solid food a week. The guardians maintained that this was more than the average independent labourer would be able to afford. However, according to *The Times* in 1842, the workhouse food allocation per inmate was about half the quantity provided for a prisoner in jail. In 1840, the Poor Law Commissioners authorised guardians to provide Christmas extras for workhouse inmates, to be paid for from the rates.

It was common practice for inmates to be given soul-destroying tasks such as stone breaking and picking oakum (from an Old English word meaning "off combings") - the picking apart of old hemp or jute rope with the aid of a spike to provide the fibres used to caulk ships. This gave rise to one of the colloquial names by which the workhouse was known - 'the spike'. The tasks were unpaid so as not to weaken the incentive to find employment outside, although payment in kind might be made in the form of extra food, tobacco and even sometimes alcohol. The aim was to encourage paupers to leave the workhouse to find employment, but workhouse officials had no powers to help inmates to find jobs. A handbook of 1871 defined the role of the workhouse whereby it *'can only extend the poor-rate in supplying the destitute with actual necessaries, such as food, clothing, or lodging ...'* In 1846, there were 1,331,000 paupers. 199,000 were in workhouses, leaving 1,132,000 subsisting on out-relief in the form of cash or kind provided by Poor Law Guardians.

As time passed there were gradual changes in the union workhouse as an institution. The intention of the 1834 Poor Law Amendment Act was that all outdoor relief to able-bodied paupers should cease except in the case of those requiring temporary relief for medical reasons. However, the provision of outdoor relief to able-bodied paupers never really ceased and the able-bodied came to make up a smaller proportion of the workhouse population from the mid 19th century onwards. By then the inmate population was frequently made up of the elderly, the sick, the infirm, unmarried mothers and children. It was intended that unmarried mothers should be isolated from other inmates as far as possible because *"their poverty was deemed to result from their moral failings"* and they were often excluded from the small privileges given to other inmates. Towards the end of the 19th century it became increasingly common practice for children to be removed from the workhouse and placed in foster homes or in separate children's homes.

By the end of the 19th century attitudes towards the causes of poverty began to change. Through the work of Charles Booth and others it was recognised that people were not necessarily unemployed and destitute because of any moral shortcomings. The extension of the right to vote allowed the election of MPs sympathetic to, and even drawn from, the working class and locally this brought about a change in the composition of boards of guardians. In 1894 the property qualification of £5 per year was abolished and voting for the election of boards of guardians was made the same as that for parliamentary elections. Working-class guardians could now be elected and women guardians became more numerous. Meetings were reported in the local press which had a rapidly growing readership, so that the guardians became accountable to a wider public.

The introduction of old age pensions in 1908 and of state sickness and unemployment insurance in 1911 were radical improvements in the quality of life for the poor. In 1913 union workhouses became known as Poor Law Institutions. In 1930 the responsibilities of the boards of guardians were placed in the hands of borough and county councils and the old workhouses were renamed Public Assistance Institutions. The Poor Law was finally replaced by the National Assistance Act of 1948.

Sources:

May, Trevor. *The Victorian Workhouse.*
1997. Shire Publications Ltd.

Reid, Andy. *The Union workhouse. A study guide for local historians and teachers.*
1994. Phillimore for British Association for Local History

Chapter 4

The Guildford Union Workhouse

"In pursuance of an Act of Parliament passed in the Fourth and Fifth years of the Reign of his present Majesty King William the Fourth intituled "An Act for the Amendment and better Administration of the Laws relating to the Poor in England and Wales," The Poor Law Commissioners for England and Wales, do hereby Order and Declare, That the Parishes and Places the names of which, and the City, County or Counties wherein they are situate, are specified in the margin of the Order, together with all Hamlets, Tythings, Liberties, or other Sub-divisions, lying within, or belonging or adjacent to, any of the said Parishes and Places, shall on the eleventh day of April next be, and henceforth shall remain, United for the Administration of the laws for the relief of the Poor, by the name of the Guildford Union, in the County of Surrey: And that a Board of Guardians of the Poor of the said Union, shall be constituted and chosen according to the provisions of the Poor Law Amendment Act, and in manner hereinafter mentioned."

1. St Nicholas)
2. St Mary's) Town of Guildford
3. Holy Trinity)
4. Albury
5. Shere
6. East Clandon
7. West Clandon
8. East Horsley
9. West Horsley
10. Merrow
11. Ockham
12. Purbright
13. Send and Ripley
14. Stoke
15. Wisley
16. Woking
17. Warplesdon
18. Wanborrow
19. Godalming
20. Compton
21. Artington

Following the Poor Law Amendment Act of 1834, an order was sent from Somerset House dated February 24th 1836 to the magistrates in Guildford instructing them to set up the Poor Law Union with an annually elected board of guardians to administer the Union. The Act went on to specify that *"The number of Guardians shall be 26, of which three shall be elected for the parish of Godalming; two each for the parishes of St Mary's (Guildford; Holy Trinity (Guildford); and Woking; and one each for the other parishes of the union. But the same person may be elected Guardian for more than one parish, agreeably to Section 40 of the Poor Law Amendment Act. Any person who shall be rated to the poor rate in some parish of the Union, in respect of hereditaments of the annual value or rental of not less than twenty pounds* [the sum has been altered by hand on the printed document to thirty pounds] .... *shall be eligible as a Guardian for any of the said parishes."*

Qualification of voters for Guardians were defined as *"Any rate payer who shall have been rated to the poor-rate in any parish in the Union for the whole year immediately preceding his voting, and shall have paid the parochial rates and assessments made on him for one whole year ....."*. *"Any owner of ratable property, situate within any parish ....."*. *"Any owner who shall be bone fide an occupier of any such property will be entitled to vote, as well as in respect of his occupation as of his being such owner."* Voters could appoint a proxy in case of necessity, provided that person fulfilled the required qualifications.

The first election was to be held on April 11th 1836. Thereafter the annual election was to be held on the first Thursday after March 25th in each year. Guardians could either be proposed (by suitably qualified rate payers or owners of property) or might propose themselves. If the number of candidates did not exceed the number of Guardians to be elected, the candidates thus proposed were declared duly elected. Should the number of candidates exceed the number of Guardians to be elected, a prescribed system of voting was to take place.

The duly elected Board of Guardians met for the first time on April 12th, 1836 at the Council Chamber in Guildford with James Mangles in the Chair pro tem. It was resolved that the Right Honourable Lord King be chairman and James Mangles be Vice President. George Shurlock Smallpeice of Guildford was appointed Clark of the Board at a salary of one hundred and thirty pounds per annum. Samuel Haydon was appointed Treasurer and he was to be required to give security to the amount of two thousand pounds. Meetings of the Board of Guardians were to take place every Saturday at ten o'clock in the morning.

Three Relieving Officers were to be appointed at the meeting of the Board of Guardians on Saturday 7th May at a salary of one hundred and twenty pounds per annum and would be required to give a security of two hundred pounds each. The sum to be paid for medical attendance to the Union was not to exceed five hundred pounds per annum. The Clerk to the Board of Guardians was to *"provide the necessary account books for the use of the union and also such other books and documents as may be required."* There was to be a report at the next meeting on the *"actual state of repairs and accommodation afforded of their respective workhouses and the number and description of their inmates."*

At the next meeting on Saturday 16th April 1836 it was resolved that a room be rented in the Abbot's Hospital for future meetings at ten pounds per annum.

The Guildford Poor Law Union consisted of about twelve square miles of South West Surrey, including 21 parishes and a population estimated at just over 21,000 in 1831 (Fig.1). Guildford and Godalming each had a population of about 4,500. It was fundamental to the new law that no out-relief should be given to the able-bodied poor but that they should be sent to the workhouse. This was intended to discourage them from seeking any relief at all and instructions of June 4th, 1836 called for the payment of out-relief to end. There was, however, a distinct reluctance on the part of the Guildford Union Guardians to cease out-relief to the able-bodied poor and send them to the workhouse as instructed. They treated the destitute with greater sympathy than many other unions and, where it was likely that a pauper was in need of temporary help and might be able to repay a loan, the Guardians were prepared to help. Funding had to be raised by rates from the parishes. In August 1836, the sum of £1,000 was raised and in December the sum of £2,500, although these calls on the parishes were exceptional. In order to raise money the Guildford workhouse in North Street was sold on August 13th, 1836. The Godalming workhouse was put up for auction in September 1838 and the Worplesdon workhouse was sold in November 1838.

The Union was divided into three districts for the work of the Relieving Officers. The Guildford District comprised Holy Trinity, St Mary's, St Nicolas (the 'h' was dropped from the saint's name in the later 19th century), Stoke, Artington, Compton, Wanborough and Godalming. The elected Relieving Officer was Timothy Lovett the younger. The Albury District comprised Albury, Shere, East Horsley, West Horsley, East Clandon, West Clandon and Merrow. The elected Relieving Officer was John Clark of Godalming. The Woking District comprised Ockham, Wisley, Woking, Send and Ripley, Worplesdon and Pirbright. The elected Relieving officer was John Parsons Kay.

For the purposes of the Medical Officers the Union was divided into six districts, who were to be paid according to the population and acreage of each district. District 1 (Guildford) comprised Holy Trinity, St Mary's, St Nicolas and Stoke at £80 per annum. District 2 comprised Artington, Compton, Wanborough and Godalming at £115 per annum. District 3 comprised Albury and Shere at £65 per annum. District 4 comprised East Horsley, West Horsley, East Clandon, West Clandon and Merrow at £65 per annum. District 4 comprised Ockham, Wisley and Send & Ripley at £75 per annum. District 6 comprised Woking, Worplesdon and Pirbright at £100 per annum. The first Medical Officers, appointed on annual contracts, were Messrs Woodyer, Stedman and Eager of Guildford for the 1st and 4th Districts; Messrs Haines, Balchin and Parsons of Godalming for the 2nd District; William Huntingdon Butler of Guildford for the 3rd District; John King Eager of Ripley for the 5th District; Edward Harbroe of Ripley for the 6th District.

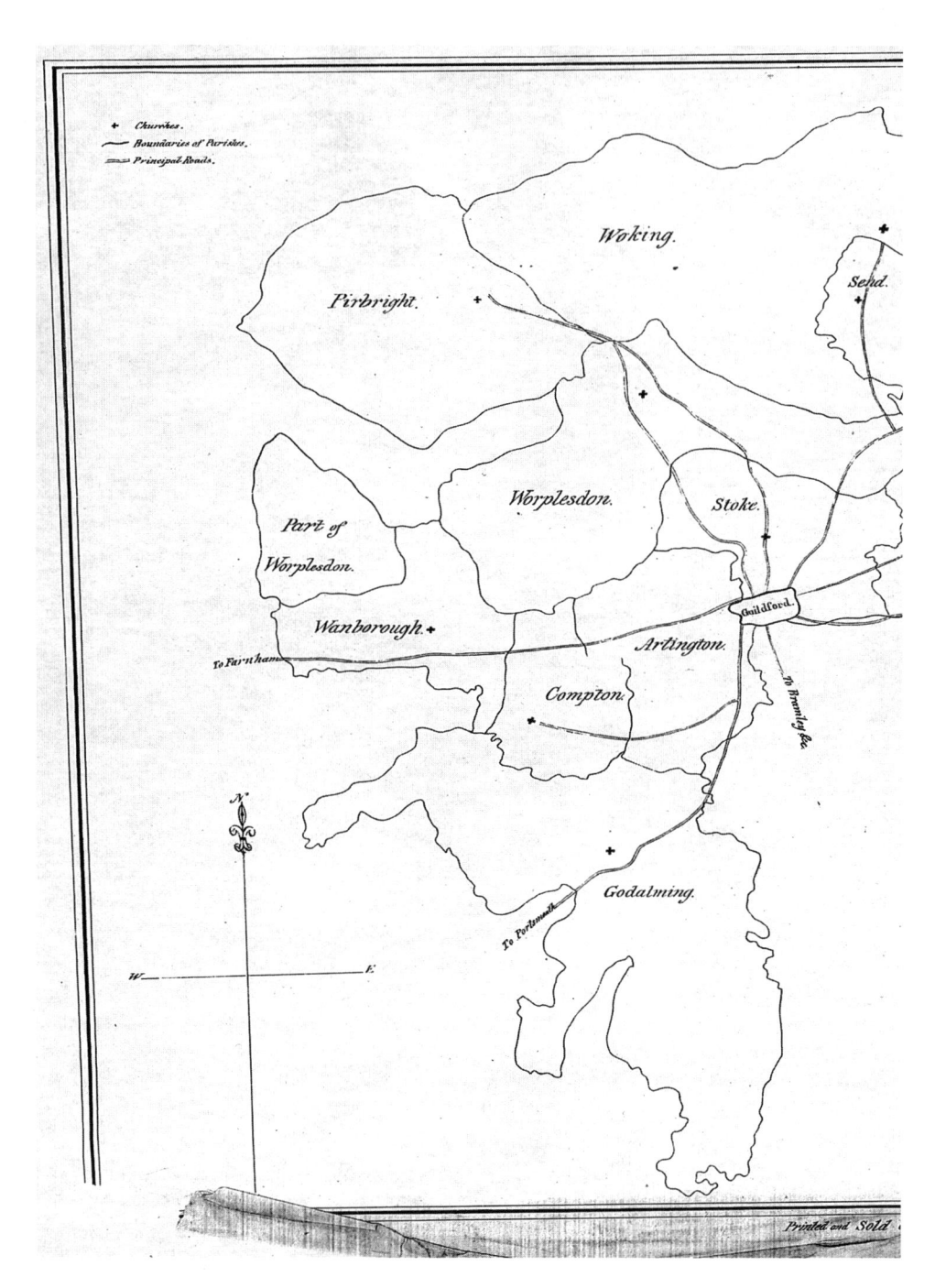

Fig.1   *Map of the Guildford Poor Law Union.*
            (By permission of Guildford Museum).

Fig.1   *Map of the Guildford Poor Law Union.*
(By permission of Guildford Museum).

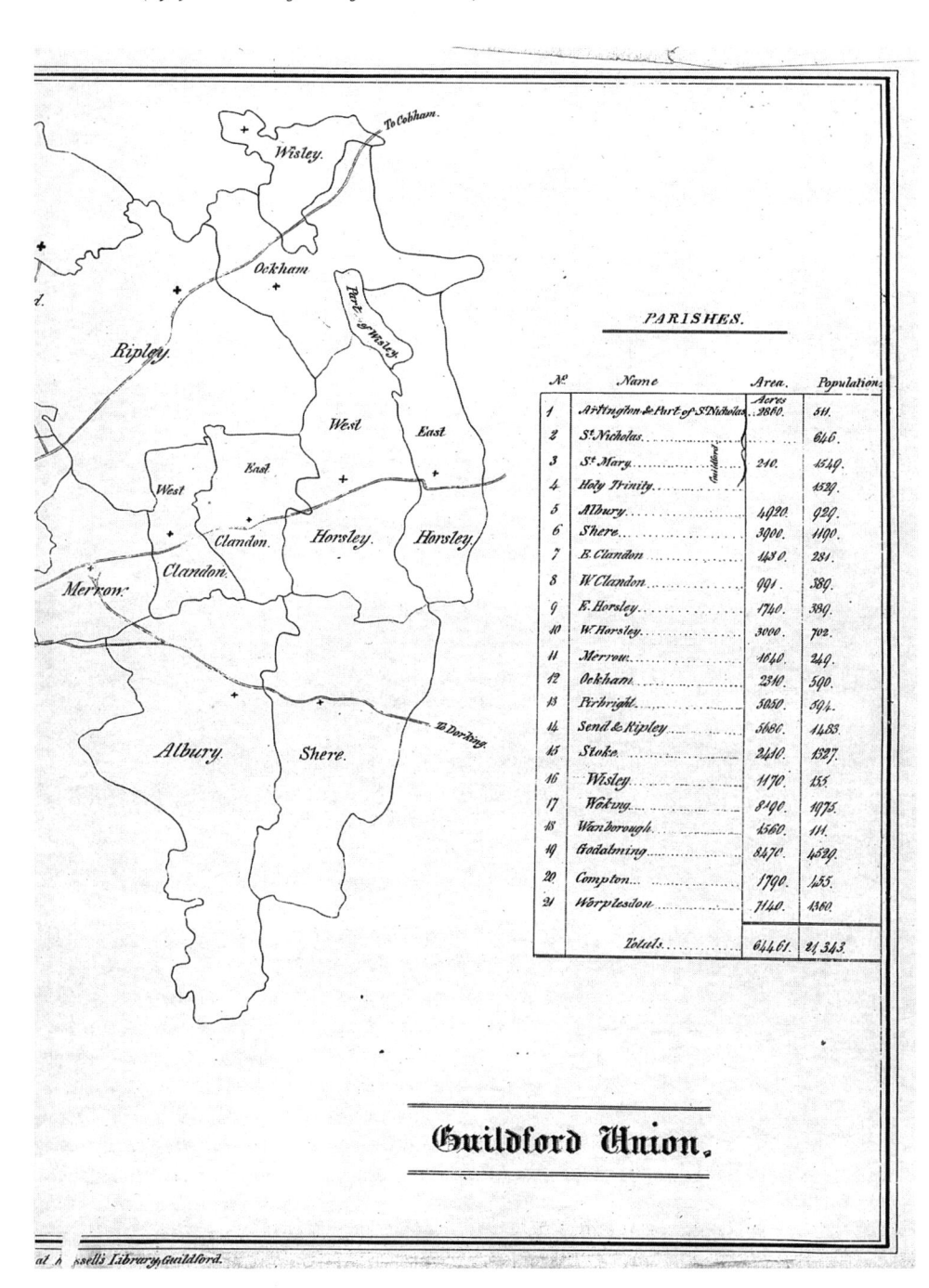

Nº	Name	Area.	Population.
		Acres	
1	Artington & Part of St Nicholas	2860.	511.
2	St Nicholas		646.
3	St Mary	240.	4549.
4	Holy Trinity		4529.
5	Albury	4020.	929.
6	Shere	3900.	1190.
7	E. Clandon	1430.	281.
8	W. Clandon	991.	389.
9	E. Horsley	1740.	389.
10	W. Horsley	3000.	702.
11	Merrow	1640.	249.
12	Ockham	2310.	590.
13	Pirbright	5050.	594.
14	Send & Ripley	5680.	1483.
15	Stoke	2410.	1527.
16	Wisley	1170.	155.
17	Woking	8490.	1975.
18	Wanborough	1560.	111.
19	Godalming	8470.	4529.
20	Compton	1790.	455.
21	Worplesdon	7140.	1360.
	Totals	64461.	21,343.

Guildford Union.

In 1841 James Stedman became Medical Officer to the Guildford Union, receiving £40 a year for medicine and attendance. From 1856 Henry Sharp Taylor was Medical Officer for the Number 1 District of the Union (Holy Trinity and St Mary) for some forty years and was well liked among the poor for his kindness and sympathy towards them. In 1858 Richard Eager was House Surgeon to the Guildford Union, a post he held until his death in 1876 when he was succeeded by Dr Charles John Sells. Also in 1858, John King Eager, possibly Richard's brother, became Medical Officer to the Union and Public Vaccinator for East and West Clandon and East and West Horsley, while Thomas Jenner Sells became Medical Officer for the Pirbright and Worplesdon areas of the Guildford Union. In about 1871 Thomas Cawley Eager was Medical Officer and Public Vaccinator for the Woking district of the Guildford Union. Charles John Sells, son of Thomas Jenner Sells, was appointed Medical Officer for the Guildford Union in 1876.

The workhouses of the joint parishes of Send and Ripley, Godalming and Worplesdon were to continue in use until a purpose-built workhouse was ready. At the meeting on Saturday 18th June 1836, it was resolved that the Board should advertise for plans and specifications and estimates for a workhouse able to take 300 paupers to be erected at Worplesdon, capable of being added to at any future time. In the meantime discussions continued at meetings on the merits of enlarging the Godalming workhouse for use as the central union workhouse or of using Worplesdon. Finally, the Board considered that a new workhouse should be built and representations were made to the Poor Law Commissioners on a number of occasions. These were rejected on the grounds that Godalming or Worplesdon workhouses should be adapted to fulfil the need.

The minutes of November 19th 1836 record that six boys were punished for absconding from the Godalming workhouse. Five were put on bread and water for a week and one was taken before the magistrates for disposing of some of the clothing issued by the Union.

In February 1837 the Board was ordered by the Poor Law Commissions that in future no gratuities or extras were to be allowed to paupers employed in washing or other work in the workhouse and that if necessary, persons from outside be hired to do such work. In addition, the Poor Law Commissions directed that the allowance of beer in the Godalming and Worplesdon workhouses to the washerwomen was illegal unless by order of the Medical Officer.

Weekly meetings were moved from Saturdays to Tuesdays. Representations continued to the Poor Law Commissioners asking for permission to construct a new purpose-built central workhouse and finally received agreement. On Tuesday 14th March 1837, the Board of Guardians resolved that William Haydon's offer of land for the construction of a new central workhouse in the parish of Stoke be accepted. The total purchase price would be £375 for six and a half acres of land. Advertisements were placed for tenders for the construction. In the event few were received and tenders by Mr Loe of Guildford for the provision of one hundred thousand red bricks at two pounds per thousand and by Mr Peacock of Godalming for the supply of one thousand loads of Bargate stone at 10s.6d per load were accepted. James Smart of Guildford was recommended as builder for the new central workhouse at the sum of £4,250. Subsequently Mr Peacock withdrew from his tender to provide the Bargate stone and Mr Smart took on that part of the contract at a revised figure of £5,360. William Haydon's land was formally conveyed to the Board of Guardians on July 18th, 1837.

Plate 1. *Illustration of the Guildford Union Workhouse. (Document PX/72/610. Reproduced by permission of Surrey History Service. Copyright of Surrey History Service).*

The architects of the Guildford Union Workhouse were George Gilbert Scott and William Bonython Moffatt, and the entrance was in Cooper Road (Plate 1). The construction work provided a source of employment for able bodied paupers. It was recorded on October 10th 1837, that a well had been sunk at the site of the new central workhouse to a depth of 53 feet. The workhouse was completed in fifteen months at a cost to the ratepayers of just under £6,000 (Fig.2). Stabling for the use of the guardians for twelve horses was added later at a cost of £90. A school and hospital accommodation were added to the workhouse in 1856. A new infirmary was built in 1893, while further additions included new dining facilities, kitchen and laundry in 1899. Finally, in 1909, a nurses home was built.

The workhouse staff included a master at £60 and a matron at £40; a chaplain at a stipend of £60 per year; a schoolmaster at £35 per year who lived in, eating the same food as the paupers; a schoolmistress at £25 per year; a porter, a nurse, a medical officer and a superintendent at £20 per year each. Inmates from the

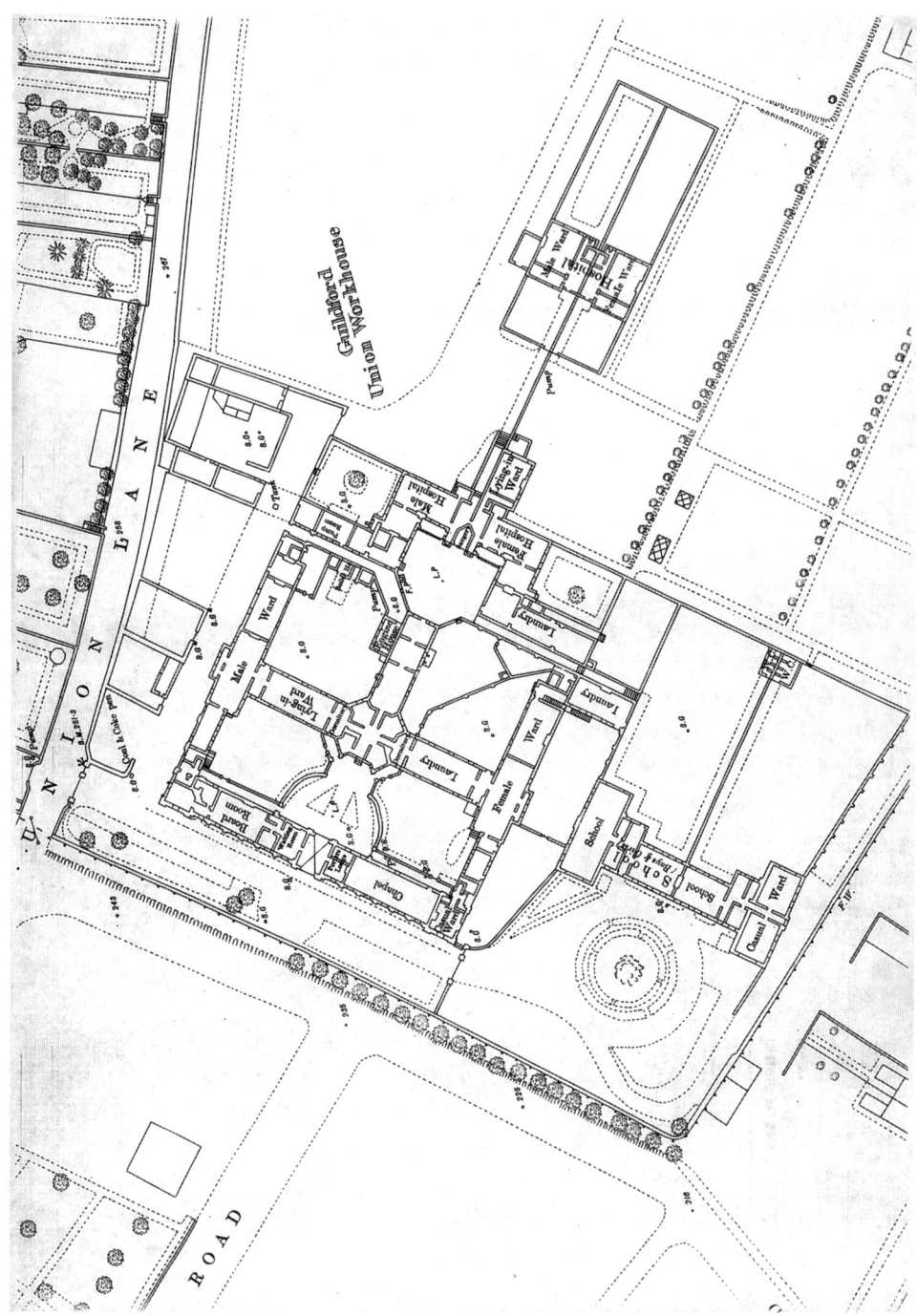

Fig.2   *Ordnance Survey map showing the Guildford Union Workhouse. (50" Sheet XXIV. 13, 21. Pub. 1871. Surveyed 1868. Reproduced by permission of Surrey History Service. Copyright of Surrey History Service).*

Godalming and Worplesdon workhouses were moved to the Guildford Union Workhouse. There was concern that the inmates should be kept occupied and in addition to wood chopping, stone crushing and oakum picking, the workhouse included a crushing mill for inmates to crush animal bone for fertilizer.

The Board of Guardians of the Guildford Union Workhouse were representatives of the area covered: Guildford, Godalming, Ockham, Wisley and Woking. The Board was given directives and permission for action by the Local Government Board, which was originally termed the Poor Law Commissioners. They dealt with rate collections, out-relief, the boarded out, lunatics, casuals (tramps), out-relief paid to other Unions for the non-resident poor, children in the Homes and at the Workhouse, the day-to-day running of the Workhouse, admissions and departures, provisions, appointments and salaries, the infirmary, schooling, labour and building. The House Committee (later called the Visiting Committee) consisted of 15 members, later increased, who met every fortnight, but visited on other days as well. Much of the initial work, especially on buildings and advertisements, was done by this committee, then debated, altered and finalised by the Board of Guardians. The Finance Committee scrutinised the expenditure of the Workhouse and the outdoor expenditure in day-to-day detail, then reported to the Board of Guardians. The Ladies' Visiting Committee, the Children's Committee, the Lunatics' Committee and the Assessment Committee all reported to the Board of Guardians. The chief officials at the Workhouse were: the Master and Matron, the Labour Master, the Medical Officer, the Chaplain, the Children's Matron, the Boys' Caretaker, the Porter and Portress, the Chief Day Nurse, the Night Nurse, the Tramp Master and Mistress.

Appendices 1-7 provide details from extracts of returns of the Board of Guardians between 1836 and 1844 relating to expenditure in providing indoor and outdoor relief, numbers relieved and medical assistance.

Suppliers to the Guildford Union remind us of many names from the past including Salsbury: clock winding; Franks: coal; Battersby: chimney sweeping; Colebrook: meat; Gammon, Hardy: clothing; Botting: corn and straw; F. Cobbett: repairs to baskets; Horstmann: spectacles; Moon: timber for repairs; Bowyer & Newell: flour; Alfred Bull: sundries; Carling Gill & Carling: ironmongery; Nicklin: clock winding; Biddle & Shippam: printing.

Sources:

Document BG6/80/1.	Reproduced by permission of Surrey History Service. Copyright of Surrey History Service.
Green, J.K.	*Sidelights on Guildford History IV.* 1956. Reprinted edition by permission of the Surrey Times.
Inglesant, George David.	*The early years of the Guildford Poor Law Union 1834-1838.* 1980. Including references from Jones, Hazel R. *A history of the Poor Law and of the parishes which formed the Guildford Poor Law Union, leading to the passing of the Poor Law Amendment Act of 1834 and until the formation of the Poor Law Board of 1847.* 1958.
May, Trevor.	*The Victorian Workhouse.* 1997. Shire Publications Ltd.

Chapter 5

The Vagrants' Casual Ward "The Spike"

The 1834 Poor Law Amendment Act made no provision for vagrants. By 1837, because so many parishes were experiencing difficulties in dealing with vagrants, the Poor Law Commissioners recommended that they should be given shelter and a meal in the workhouse in return for a job of work. From the late 1860s the idea of separate casual wards as part of workhouses was more generally promoted. In 1860 the superintendent of police reported that 30,000 tramps passed through Guildford a year, *".. doing much damage and stealing fruit, etc., from gardens"*.

The Pauper Inmates Discharge & Regulation Act of 1871 allowed workhouse guardians to detain both male and female vagrants until they had performed a morning's work. Vagrants were to be checked on entry to the workhouse for money and banned substances such as alcohol and tobacco. There was also a fear that vagrants carried disease. This was another reason for accommodating them in casual wards separate from the main workhouse inmates. On admittance they were obliged to take a bath and their clothes were disinfected. In the 1870s workhouse unions were urged to adopt a separate cell system within casual wards for vagrants which would separate them from one another, the intention being to keep them under better control. The Poor Law Board recommended that cells were to contain a bell in order to summon the Tramp Master in case of illness or trouble whilst they were locked in their cells during the night.

The 1882 Casual Poor Act laid down that all vagrants, or casuals as they came to be known, were to be detained in the casual ward for two nights. It was intended they should be given work to do on the day after their arrival and for them to leave on the following morning in time to look for employment. Tasks performed by vagrants included chopping wood, breaking stones and picking oakum. Parliamentary Reports and reports by the Poor Law Commissioners show that vagrants were always considered a danger to society. For this reason the accommodation provided in the casual wards was intended to resemble a prison and treatment was harsh. A publication entitled 'Living London', first published in 1902, includes a chapter 'In a London Workhouse' referred to as "York Palace". *"The casual ward opened at 6pm but well before that a queue of men, women, even whole families had formed. They were each questioned by the porter as to where they slept the previous night, and the usual answer was "Nowhere". Beyond the porter's lodge the men and women were divided into the separate wards. The men were next searched to see whether they possessed more money than is allowed (the limit here was 4d), and also whether they have pipes, tobacco or matches concealed about their person. After having a compulsory bath, they were given supper, consisting of one pint of gruel and 6 oz cheese. The following morning, breakfast was the same as supper. They were then set to work for the day, the women at cleaning and washing, the men at cleaning and oakum picking. The only break was for midday dinner - bread and cheese – until supper and bed. The following morning, about 36 hours after admittance, they were discharged, to return to the streets once more".* Even in the early part of the 20th century, tramps caught begging or sleeping rough were sent to gaol. Each parish was responsible for its own poor and no parish wanted tramps to care for, so the intention was to move them on as quickly and cheaply as possible. Large notices were erected at the entrances to some towns warning that any vagrant found inside the town after a certain hour would be kept overnight and appear before the magistrates the following morning.

As a result of the Local Government Board Orders of 6th April 1894 and 29th October 1895 a major building programme was instituted at the Guildford Union Workhouse. Accommodation was very crowded, especially in the children's area and the infirmary. As work went ahead on building a new dining hall, kitchen, laundry, drainage and covered corridors, the casuals (or tramps) were in temporary accommodation. Plans for new workshops and labour sheds, married couples' quarters and the new casual wards were constantly presented, discussed and amended between 1902-1904. They were postponed in March and July 1904, finally approved in December 1904 and a loan negotiated for construction.

The original contract drawings of the 'Proposed Casual Ward' dated 19th July 1872 were prepared by Henry Peak. These drawings are still held in the archive of Hodgson Lunn & Company, Chartered Architects, by John Hodgson. In February 1905 Smith & Son of Farnham Road, Guildford received the contract for laying the foundations and the basement of the new vagrants' casual ward according to the specifications of Mr E.L. Lunn, Architect, as set out in his plan dated 7th February 1905 (Fig. 3). In April 1905 Hughes of Wokingham were contracted to build the casual ward (Plate 2). However, as work progressed Guildford Corporation pointed out that no permission had been sought for new buildings. The omission was rectified with formal permission for the new vagrants' casual ward being granted on 24th June by the Town Council.

Monday 17th November

Dear Christine,

Here finally is that book on The Spike, hope you get it! Also can you give this card to Tracie for her niece's birthday in January, after I sent Lydia's birthday card in September, I found it with an extra card for Joel, I had got them both ages ago before and had forgotten all about them.

The Casual Ward p 29, 48 & 54 seems vaguely familiar; the top end is where I thought the canteen was, run by W.V.S. & the lower end an office where Dad was when he was a porter there; the corridor p 32 & 41 also bring back a sense of deja-vu!

Hope you had a good weekend, I didn't ring yesterday, didn't know what time you'd be back, but spoke to Tony Bundy who said the cheque could have gone to Perth Australia if you didn't put Scotland on the address — nothing would surprise me.

Speak to you soon
Love Tony x

Plate 2 *The Guildford Union Casual Ward.*   *(Photograph: Author).*

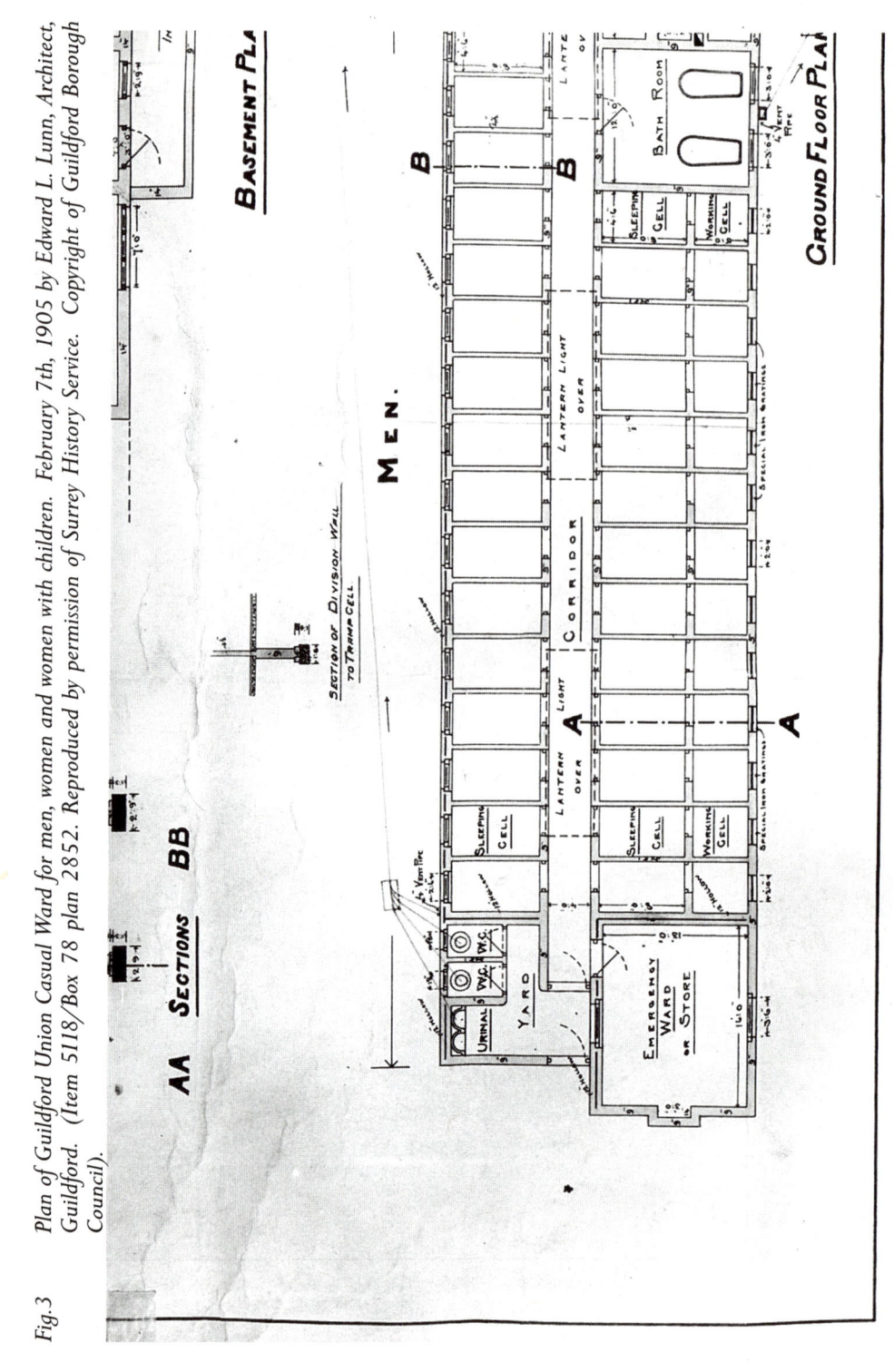

Fig.3 Plan of Guildford Union Casual Ward for men, women and women with children. February 7th, 1905 by Edward L. Lunn, Architect, Guildford. (Item 5118/Box 78 plan 2852. Reproduced by permission of Surrey History Service. Copyright of Guildford Borough Council).

Fig. 3   Plan of Guildford Union Casual Ward for men, women and women with children. February 7th, 1905 by Edward L. Lunn, Architect, Guildford. (Item 5118/Box 78 plan 2852. Reproduced by permission of Surrey History Service. Copyright of Guildford Borough Council).

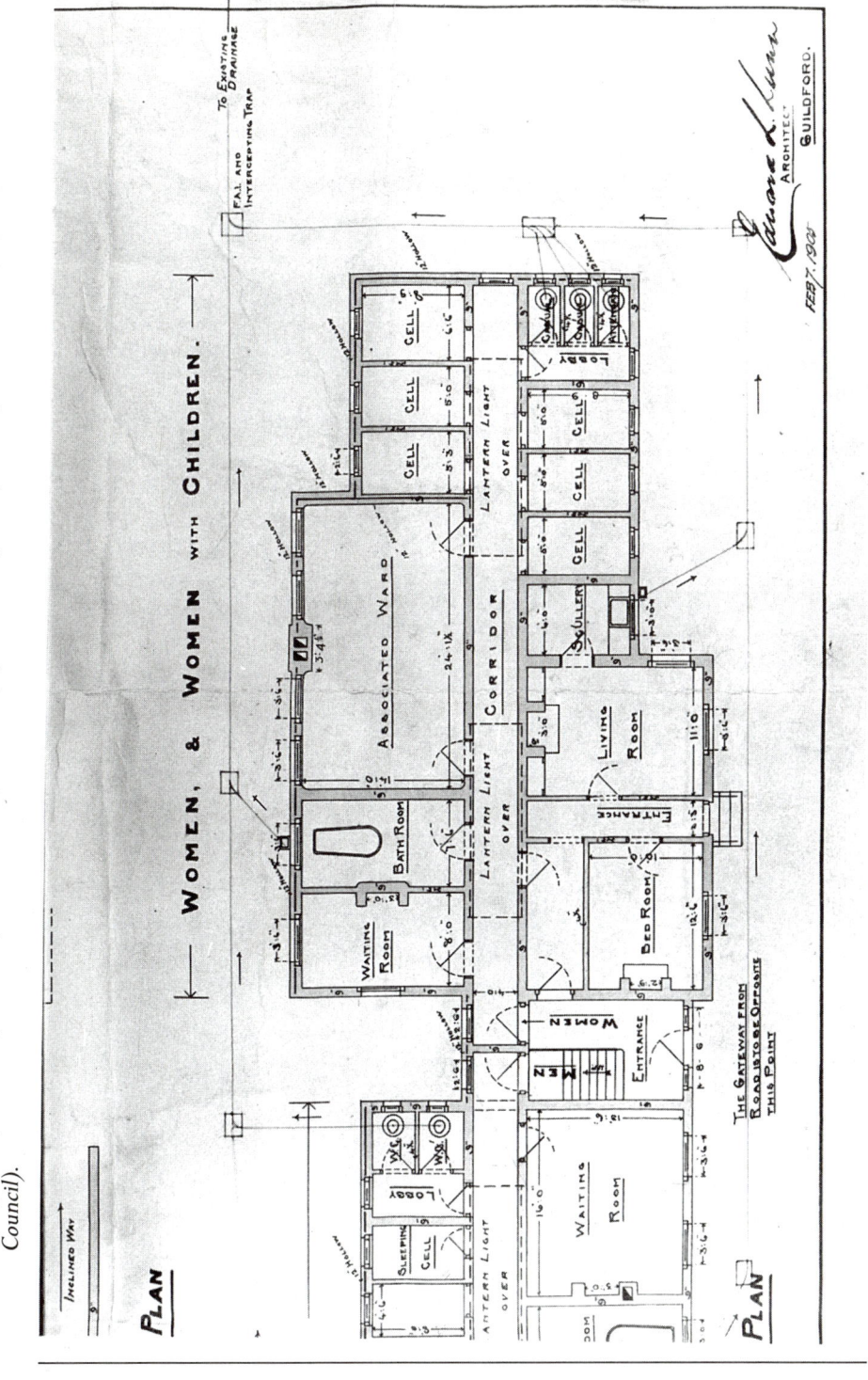

One of the requirements was that " ....*salt-glazed bricks be put in the corridors of the casual wards to the height of 4' 6"*. These were easy to wash down and keep clean (Plate 3). Glazed bricks were known as special-purpose bricks (firebricks and lightweight insulating bricks also come into this category). They were bricks with a shiny surface resulting from a secondary firing when salt was applied in the kiln to give a salt-glazed finish. These were frequently used in the 19th and early 20th centuries in situations where easy cleaning or light reflecting qualities were important, or in the hope that a glazed brick would be self-cleaning in the rain. Glazed bricks could be obtained in white or yellow enamelled finish or with a brown or red salt-glazed finish. For cleanliness alone the salt-glazed brick was adequate, for example in corridors, larders, sculleries and lavatories. Where light reflection or an alternative colour was required then twice-fired enamelled bricks were used. Simple glazed bricks were made from carefully pressed fireclay, known as refractory clay, or shale material, repressed and trimmed if necessary to give precise surfaces and sharp arrises. Fired in a downdraught kiln, or sometimes in a tunnel kiln, common salt was thrown into the kiln when a temperature of 1,200°C was reached, repeated once or twice more and the bricks allowed to cool. The salt volatilises and settles on the exposed surfaces of the bricks, the result being a mottled brown glaze, combining with the clay at the surface of the brick and is consequently more durable. (The resulting brown colour was similar to the salt-glazed stoneware used for sanitary goods such as drainage pipes). This was not a very easy type of brick to lay and a good bricklaying technique needed to be observed if a first-class finish were to be achieved. Another building in Guildford that used salt-glazed bricks, in this case as cladding for its exterior arcades, is the Rodboro Buildings on Bridge Street and the use of this type of brick is an interesting feature to look out for.

Plate 3 *Salt-glazed bricks in the corridor of the men's casual ward.*

(*Photograph reproduced by permission of David Rose*).

Plate 4 *The remaining in situ iron grills of the stone-breaking work cells, men's casual ward. (Photograph: Author).*

Mr Lunn had changed the plans for the windows of the thirteen work cells into gratings in late 1904 and was then instructed in 1905 to provide stone-breaking grids in three of the cells and wood-chopping grids in the other ten cells. The wood-chopping work cells have not survived, although there is architectural evidence for the doorways from the sleeping sections into the work cells. The wood-chopping grids have not survived either so that we have no evidence of what they look like. However, four iron grids from the stone-breaking cells survive *in situ* (Plate 4), so it would seem that there were in fact nine wood-chopping cells and four stone-breaking cells.

The contractor expected to start in June 1905 and to be finished in spring 1906. A new red brick wall was built in Warren Road between the casual ward and the road, still there today. The cell walls were to be in buff distemper. On 31st March 1906 the Board noted that the new Ideal boiler installed in the basement of the casual ward was to be insured with National Boiler & General Insurance Company for £400 at an annual premium of £1.4s.0d.

A special committee decided on furniture and fittings. Steam pipes were installed which run along the walls and through each of the cells, to provide a modicum of warmth. Pillows were ordered in May 1906 for the casual ward. There was no provision for drying vagrants' clothes but Mr Lunn felt there were several store rooms which could be used. In June 1906 Mr Lunn was asked to draw up plans for *"the provision of a store for keeping the sheets, linen and hardware used on the women's side at the new casual wards"*. This does not appear to be an external feature and it is unclear where this would have been located. Mr Lunn was also asked to provide "a temporary shelter or outside waiting room for casuals" and *"a shelter* (later called a veranda) *to the raised terrace outside the working cells"*. The waiting room (Plate 5) and the remnants of the raised terrace and veranda are still there today though unfortunately in a ruinous condition.

Plate 5   *The outside waiting room. Guildford Union Casual Ward. (Photograph: Author)*

The greater length of the veranda and raised terrace was demolished, probably round about 1938, when a storage building was constructed which is butted up to the north wall of the men's casual ward. This involved the removal of eight wood-chopping work cells. A further wood-chopping and sleeping cell was turned into a passageway with steps leading down to another small store, with a door to the right leading into the outer store and another door to the left leading out of the casual ward.

In July 1906 the casual ward was insured for £3,300 and the machinery for £200. Furniture was also to be insured. As with the rest of the workhouse, the lighting for the casual wards was by gas although in 1910 consideration was being given as to whether electricity should be introduced.

One of the work tasks for casuals was stone pounding (the crushing of flints into gravel), for which we have architectural and written evidence, and in February

1906 a tender for providing stone-pounders was accepted. In June 1906 an application was made to the Local Government Board for sanction to include *'the pounding of 100 lbs of flints for the first day of detention for male casuals'*. An advertisement was to be issued in the three local newspapers that *"Flint-pounding was now being carried out at the casual wards"* and inviting applications for the purchase *"of such grit"*. In July 1906 this was amended by the Local Government Board to *"men detained for more than one night"*. The broken stone had to be small enough to be pushed through the iron grills installed in the wall of the work cells for collection outside on the raised terrace. The crushed stone would probably have been used in road construction, although there seem to be no records referring to where the stone originated. In September 1906 prices were fixed for the sale of the flint grit at 2s.0d, 1s.9d and 1s.6d per hundredweight. Records show that two tons of flint chippings were sold for 10s.0d in November 1907 to the Borough of Godalming and a further quantity in March 1910 for 15s.0d. Three more stone-pounders were bought for £3.3s.0d each in February 1908.

Wood chopping was another task for casuals and the basement under the men's casual ward was originally intended to be largely for wood chopping, as well as in the casual working cells. Only one sale of chopped wood is recorded, in March 1909, sold for £35.14s.0d so wood chopping must have been principally to supply the workhouse. It is possible that this sale was for quality timber from the recently-cleared, newly purchased land from Lord Onslow for the Children's Receiving Wards to the east of the workhouse. There was also a wood chopping and bundling area in the new workhouse labour sheds, where workhouse inmates would have been set to work (the wood-bundling was done by a machine). The purchase of 'wood' goes on steadily in the winter months, usually in quite small amounts. However, sleepers were purchased in large numbers from October 1905 onwards and sold to the workhouse by the local railways. Haulage costs from the railway station of between £5 and £10 are recorded.

Oakum picking was certainly carried out in the workhouse and in the casual ward. Purchases from A. Godwin & Son were usually recorded three times a year and quantities were bought for example in 1900 to the value of £11.8s.9d, in 1901 for £10.11s.6d, in 1902 for £21.4s.0d, in 1903 for £55.6s.9d.

In 1901 the House Committee had decided to bake the bread at the workhouse instead of having a contract with Ayers' Bakery as this was a cheaper option and food for the casual ward was supplied from the main workhouse kitchen and (new) bakery. In October 1905 there was a suggestion that cocoa and not water should be supplied to the casuals during the winter, when many workmen would have to come in for shelter. In the Guardians' discussion, the official Diet List from the Local Government Board was read out: Supper to be 8 ounces of bread or 6 ounces of bread and one pint of gruel, with similar diets for breakfast and dinner. The master of the workhouse apparently gave 8 ounces of bread only. The Board decided to give 6 ounces of bread plus one pint of broth or gruel to all casuals over seven years of age for breakfast and supper, instead of just bread as hitherto. On one occasion in 1906, the Guardians had seen only bones put into the broth. The Tramp Master said that he had been delayed by the arrival of the Guardians from going to the kitchens and when he did, only thyme and parsley were put in, as there were no other vegetables available that day. The Guardians decided that *"in the event of the failure of the broth supply ... the master should be empowered to substitute bread as an alternative".*

All casuals were obliged to take a bath on arrival (the bathwater not being changed very frequently!). In February 1902 the House Committee decided that all tramps certified for admission into the workhouse should be put in quarantine in the isolation unit because of *"the prevalence of smallpox in London and elsewhere"*. By April Croydon Union had closed its casual wards because of smallpox in the Union and asked for this news to be posted up in Guildford. Later that month Whitmoor Cottage Hospital reported that they had a casual who had recently been in Guildford, who must have shown the symptoms of smallpox there. However, Guildford found a witness in a fellow casual who testified that the man had shown no signs of the disease when he was bathed. In April 1903 smallpox was again prevalent in Surrey and precautions were taken to isolate suspects. The Local Government Board was concerned that casuals were spreading the disease. When the new casual ward was built, a large room at the east end of the men's casual ward was designed to be used as an infirmary when necessary.

The posts of Tramp Master and Mistress for the new casual ward are not mentioned in the minutes of meetings until the advertisements for the appointments are discussed by the Guardians in October 1905. However, when the new Porter and Portress were appointed in January 1905, the Porter was also to be Assistant Relieving Officer of Vagrants at £5.0s.0d per annum. The post of Chief Relieving Officer of Vagrants is not separately mentioned in the records at all. Mr Staunton, the new Porter, had originally been Labour Master at Guildford before going to Maidenhead Union.

In November 1905 the House Committee noted the pressure on existing staff in the workhouse. There was to be extra help to the Porter between 6-9pm pending other arrangements being made for casuals. In December 1905, advertisements were to be placed for the posts of Tramp Master and Mistress at salaries of £25 and £20 per annum respectively. A knowledge of tailoring or shoemaking was a preference for men. There were to be free rations, living quarters and laundry. The Tramp Mistress would be provided with a uniform, in the same way as the other female officers in the workhouse. The uniform for the Tramp Master and other workhouse officers consisted of a patrol jacket, waistcoat, two pairs of trousers, cap and overcoat, to be renewed yearly except for the overcoat, which was to be renewed every three years. The uniform was to be the property of the Guardians for the first six months and the overcoat for always.

Plate 6. *Entrance to accommodation for Tramp Master and Mistress. Guildford Union Casual Ward. (Photograph: Author)*

On 13th January 1906 it was decided to appoint Mr G. Kent, the Boys' Caretaker, and Miss Tomlinson, the Cook, as Tramp Master and Mistress as long as they were married first. They were granted six days' absence in March. Mr Bassett, the Baker, took on the additional duty of Cook in Mrs Kent's place. The Tramp Master and Mistress took up their posts in late March or early April 1906 and one of the first tasks of the Tramp Master was to have the name 'Guildford Union Casual Wards' painted on the outside wall in late April. (There is no evidence for this signage on the walls of the casual wards today). Mrs Kent was supplied with a sewing machine, a Singer, at £7.11s.0d. In May 1906 Mr and Mrs Kent's salaries were raised to £42.0s.0d and £39.0s.0d respectively. In September 1906 a Testimonial was granted to them and in May 1907, Mr Kent arranged for a substitute during his fourteen-day holiday at £1.0s.0d per week. On 7th December 1907 Mr and Mrs Kent resigned with effect from 30th December and a temporary Tramp Master was to be appointed. By 28th December, twenty-eight applications had been received and in January 1908, Mr and Mrs Judd were appointed.

On 8th August 1908 the House Committee decided to change the job description of the Tramp Master in any future advertisement from 'tailoring and shoemaking' to 'cultivation of land' (land was cultivated at the workhouse and new piggeries were to be built). A week later the Judds gave in their resignations. Had the extra pressures in June and July been responsible, when £1.0s.0d each was granted to the Tramp Master and the Porter for five weeks' extra duties following the resignation of the Labour Master, or was it to seek promotion (but no testimonial had been asked for)? When they left, the Judds were not allowed to keep their uniforms. On 5th September, Mr and Mrs Vout of London were appointed. They had a child and it was recommended that the sum of 1s.6d a week should be charged for its maintenance. In December, £3 per annum was fixed as the value of the uniform of the Tramp Master, Porter, Labour Master and Male Infirmary Attendant.

The accommodation for the Tramp Master and Mistress built into the 1904-05 plans for the casual wards was between the men's and the women's wards, at the east end of the women's block and west of the main entrance. It had its own entrance door, with steps and iron railings (Plate 6), a hallway, bedroom, sitting room and scullery, all of which can still be seen. There was also a tiny garden in front of the accommodation with decorative edging, the remnants of which are still there. It was minuted in June 1907 that the apartments were to be plastered and whitewashed. In August 1907 the House Committee decided that an internal telephone should be linked from the Master's house to the casual wards.

In 1906 the annual salaries of workhouse officers were recorded as follows:

Tramp Master	£42
Tramp Mistress	£39
Labour Master	£25 rising to £30
Porter	£25 rising to £30
Portress	£20 rising to £25
Charge Night Nurse	£32 rising to £36
The Day Nurse	£28 rising to £33
Assistant Nurses	£21 rising to £28
Master over 3 years service	£100 rising to £115
Matron over 3 years service	£50 rising to £65
Ward maid	£17 rising to £21
Chaplain	£100

The officers' weekly rations in September 1907 were set as follows:

Meat	7lbs	Bread	5 lbs
Bacon	1lb	Vegetables	7lbs
Butter	3/4lb	Currants	1/2lb
Tea	1/4lb	Milk	7 pints
Loaf sugar	1lb	Eggs	4

Although terms like 'detention' could be used for casuals even for a one-night stay, the House Committee and Board of Guardians were alert to complaints of ill-treatment by casuals and by the public on their behalf. In May 1906 the House Committee discussed the concern of the Woking Guardians about the treatment of casuals. A letter was received concerning a conversation overheard between the Tramp Master and a casual, in which the Tramp Master used indecent language. The Tramp Master in a written reply denied this, but it was decided that he had lost his temper and would be cautioned. In March 1908 a casual complained that the Porter had kicked him several times on his discharge.

After investigation the Porter was exonerated. In September 1908 two men in the casual wards were granted a pair of boots each, as their own were worn out. In July 1910 the Tramp 'Superintendent' was accused by the Guildford District Relieving Officer of refusing entry to a casual but was exonerated because the casual had not actually applied.

In February 1901 it was considered inadvisable to discharge casuals on Sunday mornings, and other Surrey Unions agreed. In October 1901 the chaplain had arranged to hold a weekly service for casuals in reply to the Tramps Mission enquiry. In October/November 1906 the House Committee considered allowing the casuals to foregather in the large wards on Sundays, but this was refused, except for a religious service. Books and papers were placed in their cells. In November 1907 Miss Onslow, a member of the Board of Guardians, asked and received permission to supply copies of the *Daily Mail* each week to the casual wards. The Tramps Mission offered a small library of Bibles, Gospel literature and wall cards for the casual wards, which were accepted with thanks.

In November 1903 the Staines Union sent a circular expressing concern about the children of casuals. The State Children's Association sent a circular with the print of a Bill *'for the better protection of vagrant children'* but there is otherwise no mention in any minutes of the children of vagrants.

On occasions casuals were brought before the Justices of the Peace or were otherwise disciplined. In June 1900 there was a circular from Coventry Union asking if other Unions detained casuals for seven days. No particular action or response was made by the Board. On 22nd December 1906 a man was sentenced to twenty one days hard labour for smashing four panes of glass and a bedstead at the casual wards on 15th December. On 28th March 1907 two casuals were sentenced by Guildford Justices of the Peace to twenty-one and fourteen days respectively. In July 1909 the House Committee referred to the *"..... question of the number of cases recently taken before Justices from the [Guildford] Tramp Wards and desire to point out that out of 4,479 admissions during the past year, there have only been 19 prosecutions and in no instance was the case dismissed by the Justices, which would show that the action of the Master in sending the cases to the Justices was justified"*.

Even before the vagrants' casual ward was built, stone pounding was a noisy and backbreaking task that had to be carried out by workhouse inmates. The memoirs of Eli Hamshire, written in 1884, recount how he *"then went up Sydney Road and Austen Road where I heard them punching flints into a powder, for the roads round the Union, which is of very little value. I have often thought that it must be a nuisance to the people living around the Union to hear the iron bars chinking, and how much better it would be if these institutions were placed on waste land, so that they might cultivate it, as we have thousands of acres that would pay well for cultivating, and be the means of lessening the Poor Rate, there being so many of the public unable to pay it at the present time"*. Indeed complaints are recorded from neighbours with properties in close proximity of the casual ward on various issues. In June 1906 a letter of complaint was received from a neighbour living opposite the casual ward about a woman screaming. After inquiry the House Committee agreed that no blame was attributable to the workhouse. In July 1906 the same neighbour complained about the noise of hammering at the casual ward. This problem was further borne out when a local resident visited the vagrants' casual ward on Heritage Open Day in September 1999 and told me how she remembered as a child in 1932 hearing the clink of stones being hammered. She also remembered hearing screaming emanating from the workhouse. In March 1907 there were complaints of a 'nuisance' caused by smoke from a chimney pot at the casual wards. In September 1907 there was a protest from the residents of Albury Road, Upper Edgeborough Road and Warren Road over the purchase of land next to the workhouse in Warren Road from Lord Onslow for the Children's Receiving Wards. In April 1908 Guildford Chamber of Trade also protested, as did the Ratepayers and Property Owners Association. In January 1909 a letter was received from a resident of Austen Road complaining *"of a disturbance at the Tramp Wards on Sunday night last"*. The response by the House Committee after discussion was to inform the workhouse master at once. In July 1909 a resident of Warren Road was concerned about the treatment of tramps in reference to the noises heard and complained of by him.

Plate 7. Entrance to Guildford Union Casual Ward from Warren Road. The corner of the roof of the outside waiting room can be seen bottom right.
(Photograph: by permission Peter and Val Harfleet)

The entrance to the vagrants' casual ward was from Warren Road, on the north side of the building and the entrance gate is still there with the remains of a gas lamp above (Plate 7) although this entrance is now inaccessible.

At the east end of the men's casual ward, in what is now the present-day entrance, was a walled yard with two urinals and two WCs. The two urinals were located in what is now the doorway into the building. This end of the building was redeveloped in about 1938 when the Public Assistance Institution Infirmary became the Warren Road Hospital. The two WCs were enclosed within the building. One additional WC cubicle and three washbasins were added with a Sadia hot water tank in what were originally two sleeping cells (on the left as one proceeds along the corridor). The yard was covered in and a small extension constructed to the right of the modern entrance. The two urinals were moved into the extended area with one additional WC cubicle and two washbasins. Originally a window from the 'emergency ward or store' gave onto the yard. The window frame can still be seen on the inside of the 'emergency ward or store' but the window was filled in when the yard was enclosed and the sanitary extension added. The room would have been used as an emergency ward for sick vagrants. A door beneath an archway would have given access to the yard and sanitary facilities from the casual ward corridor. Inside the doorway, twenty one brick stretchers form an arched entrance, with a line of twenty headers above. Evidence of door fixings in the wall on either side of the interior of the corridor can be seen.

Plate 8. *The corridor in the men's casual ward showing cells on either side. (Photograph by permission of David Rose)*

The central corridor is 4ft wide (Plate 8) with a stone floor. There were two further WCs at the west end of the corridor which have unplastered, painted brick walls. On the walls of the corridor there is evidence of electrical wiring and switches, with a switch between each cell.

The building was designed to resemble a prison with its cells in which the occupants were locked and bolted. In total there were 30 single occupancy cells, 17 sleeping cells on the south side of the building and 13 sleeping plus work cells on the north side. The sleeping and work cells were divided by an inner wooden door (Plate 9). Four of these cells remain *in situ*, just as they were when they were last used. There is a step down into each work cell which has a small wooden bench seat and a heavy iron grill 2ft wide (Plate 10). These iron grills were unhooked and lowered from the raised platform outside, the quantity of stone to be broken was dumped in the work cell and the grill locked in place (Plate 11). The four remaining grills and remainder of the raised platform can still be seen. The dimensions of the sleeping cells on the south side are eight feet by four feet six inches (8ft x 4ft 6ins). On the north side the sleeping cells are 8ft x 4ft 6ins and the working cells 5ft by 4ft 6ins. The individual cell walls have been plastered. However, on the south side, in the third cell along the corridor for some unknown reason the brick walls have been left unplastered, although painted in the same manner as the other cells. Inside each of the cells, on the wall flush with the door frame, there is evidence of electrical wiring and a switch.

At night the casuals were locked and bolted into their cells. A few of the original sturdy wooden cell doors remain *in situ* which allow us to see where the heavy lock and a series of bolts were fitted (Plate 12). Each door had a spy-hole (Plate 13) - and a certain amount of graffiti on the interior of the some of the doors, some of it quite rude! (Plate 14).

When the Casual Ward was built, it was resolved that *"The cells will be provided with inlet and outlet ventilators in accordance with the Local Government Board Regulations"*. These ventilators can be seen beside the windows and just above floor level in each cell. The cell windows could be opened by means of a rope pulley system. The remnants of one of these pulley systems can still be seen in one of the cells on the south side. Hot water pipes run through each of the cells, which offered a token amount of heating in cold weather.

Salt-glazed bricks were used along the lower part of the corridor walls. Above each cell door, twelve curved bricks form an archway. The bricks above the salt-glazed level are unglazed but smooth and painted light green. These smooth bricks were known as 'commons', used for all internal walling prior to being plastered or painted, and were probably produced by the Fletton industry. From the last decade of the nineteenth century, developments in the mechanisation and mass production of brick manufacture allowed the Oxford clay measures across Buckinghamshire, Bedfordshire and Cambridgeshire to be exploited. The

Oxford clay discovered in 1881 at Fletton near Peterborough, had a quality, depth and uniformity of formations which gave it unique advantages for brickmaking. The green bricks were strong enough to be stacked in the kiln immediately and a five percent natural fuel content meant the clay itself would burn thus reducing fuel cost by two thirds in the firing process. These advantages, together with advances in brick production, contributed to Flettons being recognised as commodity bricks, setting the pricing standard for the industry as a whole.

Plate 9. Wooden door between sleeping and work cell in men's casual ward.
(photograph by permission of Victor Beard)

Plate 10. Interior of sleeping cell leading into stonebreaking cell, men's casual ward.
(Photograph by permission of Victor Beard)

Plate 11. Interior of stone-breaking work cell showing iron grill. (Photograph by permission of Peter and Val Harfleet)

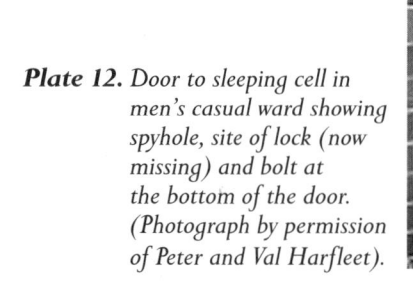

Plate 12. Door to sleeping cell in men's casual ward showing spyhole, site of lock (now missing) and bolt at the bottom of the door. (Photograph by permission of Peter and Val Harfleet).

Plate 13. Inside of door in men's casual ward sleeping cell showing spyhole.
(photograph by permission of David Rose)

Plate 14. Graffiti on the inside of one of the cell doors, men's casual ward.
(Photograph by permission of David Rose)

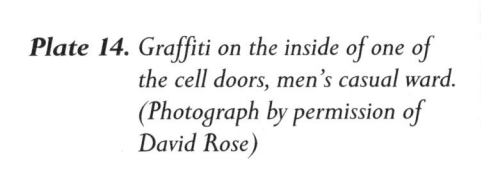

On the north wall outside the bathroom and waiting room are the remains of two rows of clothes hooks fixed onto wooden boards. On admittance vagrants were obliged to take a bath and their clothes were disinfected and left to hang in the corridor. This was because of the fear that vagrants carried disease. In the bathroom there were two baths and part of the tile surround is still there in the north-east corner of the room. The bathroom measured 13ft 6ins x 12ft with two 3ft windows. Next to the bathroom is the waiting room with a fireplace on the east wall. The waiting room also served as the dining room where meals were taken and where on Sunday church services were held.

After the Vagrants' Casual Ward closed in 1962, the building was used for storage by St Luke's Hospital. A false ceiling was inserted above the corridor although originally the corridor was lit by lantern lights and would have been open to the roof (Plate 15). The lantern lights were subsequently removed because of water leakage.

Plate 15. A picture taken in April 1963 showing the lantern lights in situ, above the casual ward.
(Photograph by permission of John Adams)

Plate 16. A picture taken in 1962 showing tramps queuing outside the casual ward.
(Photograph by permission of John Adams)

Plate 17. The door that led into the men's casual ward.
(Photograph: Author 1999)

Vagrants queued along the pavement outside the entrance and waited for the gate to open at 6pm (Plate 16). There was a waiting room just inside the gate, to the left against the brick wall, where the vagrants were then assembled. There they would have been checked for banned items such as tobacco, matches and alcohol. If they had more than four pence, they were turned away. They were then admitted into the building, the men climbing the stairs to the male casual ward (Plate 17), the women turning right into the female casual ward. There were stories told of tramps hiding money and tobacco behind the large stones in the wall opposite the casual ward in Warren Road before queuing for admittance, which they would retrieve when they left (Plate 18). Obviously they ran the considerable risk, since the habit was well known, of losing their hidden possessions to others who knew where to look. But not all the hidden cash was retrieved. During the first Heritage Open Day in September 1999, one of our visitors told me that, when her stone wall on Warren Road was repaired many years ago, the sum of five shillings was discovered hidden behind one of the stones.

Plate 18. Warren Road, Guildford. The casual ward is on the right. Opposite are stone walls in which tramps hid money etc. (Photograph: Author)

Beneath the casual ward are basement rooms built into the terraced ground levels which provided storage rooms, a wood sawing and chopping room and a boiler room. These are not accessible but do resemble the plan of 1905. There was an inclined way leading into the basement on both the north and south side of the building. From the exterior of the building it is possible to distinguish the actual floor level of the male casual ward by following the line of the lower inlet/outlet ventilators. The basement rooms can be seen below this level. On the south side of the building, another door can be seen between the male and female casual ward which gives access to the two parts of the building. This is situated immediately opposite the main Warren Road entrance and was presumably used as a staff entrance to the casual ward.

The casual ward for women and women with children was housed at the west end of the building (Plate 19). This was used as office accommodation by St Luke's Hospital staff and later by Crest Homes Ltd. as their site office and was not normally accessible. However, the writer was allowed brief access and in fact the interior of the building closely resembles the plan of 1905. From that plan, it will be seen that the women's casual ward was much smaller with six sleeping cells, suggesting that there were fewer female vagrants to be accommodated, a waiting room, a bathroom with one bath, three WCs and an 'associated ward' that was probably used as a sick ward.

Plate 19. The women's casual ward at the west end of the building. (Photograph: Author 1999)

Many of the new hospitals that evolved from the original workhouse infirmaries continued to maintain their vagrants' casual wards, which became known as reception centres, into the 1960s. Thus, when the Guildford Union Workhouse, then a Public Assistance Institution, evolved into the Warren Road Hospital and subsequently St Luke's Hospital, it too maintained its vagrants' casual ward as a reception centre. The reception centre closed in 1962 (Plate 20).

Plate 20. *A picture taken later in 1962 of the entrace to the casual ward in Warren Road, now closed.*
(Photograph by permission of John Adams)

Sources:

BG6/11/29, 30, 31, 32, 33, 34, 35. Minutes of the Board of Guardians.
BG6/12/2. Minutes of the Finance Committee.
BG6/12/7,8,9. Minutes of the House (later Visiting) Committee.
CC767/22/8/1. South East Counties Joint Vagrancy Committee.
Reproduced by permission of Surrey History Service. Copyright of Surrey History Service.

Brunskill, R.	*Brick Building in Britain.* Paperback Edition 1997. Victor Gollanz.
Gould, J.	*Old Merrow.* 1948. Facsimile re-print with additional notes. Peter Knee. Merrow, Guildford. 1988. *Living London.* First published 1902. Cassell & Co. Ltd. Reprinted as *Edwardian London,* 1990. The Village Press Ltd
Lynch, Gerard C.J.	*Brickwork. History, Technology and Practice Volume 1.* 1994. Donhead Publishing Ltd.
Stemp, David.	*Three Acres and a Cow. The Life and Works of Eli Hamshire.* 1995.

Chapter 6

From Union Workhouse to St Luke's Hospital

The original Guildford Union Workhouse sick wards were replaced by a Poor Law Infirmary known as the Guildford Infirmary (sometimes referred to as the Guildford Union Infirmary) which was opened in 1896. The minutes of the Guildford Board of Guardians of 1891 record that the Guardians were tardy in setting up the infirmary and were prompted to do so by an unfavourable report on their existing sick wards by a medical inspector from the Local Government Board.

During the First World War, part of the workhouse (by then known as a Poor Law Institution) and the infirmary were combined to form a military hospital (Plates 21 and 22). These two pictures show the entrance to the workhouse in Cooper Road. The entrance and the original workhouse buildings were demolished in 1965/66 following a severe fire in the out-patients' building. The infirmary was administered by the Guildford Guardians until 1930, when it was taken over by Surrey County Council following the Local Government Act of 1929 and at that time the infirmary had one hundred and ninety beds, including five maternity beds. It continued primarily as a Poor Law Infirmary until 1938 when it was designated a general hospital and placed under the control of the County Council's Public Health Committee and named the Warren Road Hospital. An annexe of huts was built in 1939 for Second World War casualties.

The name of the Warren Road Hospital was changed in 1945 to St Luke's Hospital after the nearby Mission Church of St Luke's in Addison Road and the patron saint of physicians. In 1948 St Luke's Hospital was incorporated into the National Health Service as an acute general hospital with 425 beds. There were tentative plans for a large modern hospital on the Warren Road site. However, when planning for a new district general hospital began in 1967 the site was no longer considered suitable for such a purpose.

In January 1980 general hospital services were transferred to the new Royal Surrey County Hospital. St Luke's Hospital continued to offer specialised services and expanded facilities for training nurses until 1991 when the hospital joined with the Royal Surrey County Hospital to form a joint self-governing trust within the National Health Service. Part of the hospital site was used by the University of Surrey's European Institute of Health & Medical Sciences (EIHMS) which then moved to purpose-built facilities on the university campus in September 1999. It was now the end of the road for St Luke's Hospital.

Plate 21. *The infirmary and part of the workhouse in use as Guildford Military Hospital during the First World War, showing the workhouse entrance.*
(Postcard reference number 67923 from Folio 9A Guildford Photograph Album Number 4. Page 17. Guildford Military War Hospital.
Reproduced by permission of Surrey History Service.
Copyright of Surrey History Service.)

The site was acquired for redevelopment as housing and, in 1997, the first phase of construction saw the creation of St Luke's Square. One low range of buildings, known as 'The Maids' House' and dating from a phase of extensions of about 1896-8 at the workhouse, has been retained and incorporated into the new development. In 1999 the annexe of huts was demolished and redeveloped as St Luke's Park. By 2003 the transformation of the site was complete with not a trace remaining of what had existed before - apart from one rare surviving building.

It was on 3rd December 1998 that the writer made a fortuitous visit to the European Institute of Health & Medical Sciences for a day's First Aid course. During lunch a chance conversation about the union workhouse with one of the staff led to the discovery of the Vagrants' Casual Ward. The men's casual ward was being used as a store and the women's casual ward as offices by the hospital

(Plate 23). I was taken over to the building and given the opportunity to look inside the men's casual ward - and could not believe what I was seeing. Following my visit, permission was generously given to record the interior and exterior of the building.

Plate 22. *The Infirmary and part of the workhouse in use as Guildford Military Hospital during the First World War, showing the workhouse entrance.*
(Postcard reference number 67924 from Folio 9A Guildford Photograph Album Number 4. Page 17. Guildford Military War Hospital. Reproduced by permission of Surrey History Service.
Copyright of Surrey History Service).

Although the Guildford Union Workhouse and St. Luke's Hospital have vanished, the Vagrants' Casual Ward was saved from demolition and granted Grade II Listed status in November 1999 as a result of the efforts of a few dedicated individuals (Fig.4). The building is still owned by the developers and the women's casual ward at the west end of the building continued in use as offices for the construction staff until completion of the housing construction project. Now the casual ward stands empty and is falling into disrepair whilst a use is sought for what is an extraordinarily difficult building to convert without destroying its unique identity. Since 1999 the casual ward has been opened to the public as part of Heritage Open Weekend, thanks to the generosity of the owners and has proved an unexpectedly popular attraction. Visitors have discovered a building unlike anything they could have imagined or are ever likely to see again. The Vagrants' Casual Ward of the Guildford Union Workhouse is an extremely rare surviving example, its very survival an extraordinary stroke of chance. Its identity and history remained virtually unknown until its rediscovery in 1998 and it stands as a memorial to those given shelter within the union workhouse.

Plate 23. *A picture taken in 1999 showing the west end of the casual ward on the left. The building on the right was part of St. Luke's Hospital, since demolished. (Photograph: Author)*

The workhouse stood in what were essentially beautiful surroundings with extensive views over the countryside which today make the new housing development much sought after. But, for the inmates of the workhouse and the casual wards, there was no beauty to be found in the surroundings and the accommodation was the last place on earth they would have wished to occupy. What a difference time and redevelopment have created.

Sources:

Brooking, Charles. Architectural Historian. (Personal communication)
Davies, Paul M. *The South West Surrey Hospitals 1859-1991.*
A Short Outline of their Origins and Development.
1993. South West Surrey Health Authority.

SCHEDULE

The following building shall be added to the list:

TQ 04 NW	GUILDFORD	WARREN ROAD
1688/4/10015		"Vagrants Casual Ward" at St. Luke's Hospital
		II

Vagrants casual ward, later used as store. 1905, Architect E L Lunn. A purpose-built vagrants ward added to Guildford Union Workhouse. Minor alterations of 1935 and late C20. Built of red brick with tiled roof with four large cemented rooflights and four brick chimneystacks. One storey. West part of south front was used as day room, dining room and for Sunday chapel services and has 6 sash windows with four glazing bars to upper part and verticals only to lower parts and lower section with two small windows and door approached by fire escape. Gable end has brick vertical pattern, West end was the cell block with 18 small cell windows and similar pattern to gable end. 1935 toilet block at east end. North elevation has four iron grills remaining out of an original thirteen which are an extremely rare survival. Each working cell had a sleeping cell and a working cell with a wooden door between the two parts of the cell. The iron grill was opened from the exterior, the load of stone to be crushed was dumped inside the working cell, the grill closed and inmates were made to crush the stone into small enough pieces to be pushed through the grill into collection containers outside. The interior retains the plan with central corridor lined with salt glazed bricks to the lower part, wooden seats to sleeping cells and spyholes to doors of sleeping cells.

Signed by authority of the
Secretary of State

T A ELLINGFORD
Department for Culture, Media and Sport

Dated: 16 November 1999

Fig. 4   The Department for Culture, Media and Sport Listing of the Guildford Union Casual Ward, 16th November 1999.
(Reproduced from author's own copy).

Appendix 1 Guildford Union. Extract from the Quarterly Abstract for the Quarter ending 24th September, 1836

GUILDFORD UNION.

Extract from the QUARTERLY ABSTRACT, shewing the number of Paupers relieved, the Amount of Money expended, and the Balances due to and from the several Parishes, for the Quarter ending 24th September, 1836.

PARISHES.	In-door Adults Males	In-door Adults Females	In-door Children	Out-door Adults Males	Out-door Adults Females	Out-door Children	GRAND TOTAL	EXPENDITURE Proportion of In-Maintenance £ s. d.	Out-Relief £ s. d.	Proportion of Establishment Charges £ s. d.	TOTAL £ s. d.	Balance due to the Parish £ s. d.	Balance due from the Parish £ s. d.
Artington	5	4	3	18	29	86	145	16 19 3	65 13 11	7 6 2	89 19 4	13 3 11	—
Saint Nicholas	2	5	4	18	34	40	103	10 1 1	74 5 0	5 16 10	90 2 11	—	10 15 8
Saint Mary	4	3	3	15	17	7	42	16 18 1	46 6 0	4 8 0	67 12 1	—	5 2 11
Holy Trinity	2	2	3	18	30	66	119	8 9 6	53 12 0	7 2 4	69 3 10	80 19 2	—
Albury	8	3	1	33	43	68	156	16 18 11	95 14 6	10 11 11	122 15 4	84 2 2	—
Shere	—	1	—	6	2	—	9	2 0 0	5 12 0	0 12 7	8 4 7	1 4 5	—
East Clandon	—	—	—	7	8	16	31	—	36 7 6	1 19 8	38 7 2	—	8 10 5
West Clandon	—	—	—	5	8	16	29	—	28 13 0	1 6 9	29 19 9	—	9 10 3
East Horsley	1	—	1	14	23	30	69	4 0 3	61 4 4	3 16 2	69 0 9	—	11 12 9
West Horsley	—	—	2	7	14	30	53	4 0 2	26 11 6	1 14 6	32 6 2	—	6 6 5
Merrow	6	—	1	2	11	16	43	10 5 9	34 7 0	3 9 5	48 2 2	4 11 4	—
Ockham	1	1	4	12	11	33	62	8 11 11	40 16 6	3 9 7	52 18 0	0 14 9	—
Pirbright	2	5	6	43	49	130	235	25 8 11	130 7 6	11 1 8	166 18 1	1 5 5	—
Send and Ripley	1	1	5	27	44	106	184	13 6 10	113 11 6	7 19 1	134 17 5	—	28 9 8
Stoke	—	—	—	3	3	13	19	—	7 8 0	1 2 6	8 10 6	8 9 0	—
Wisley	6	3	11	46	51	131	248	29 15 1	114 12 4	13 0 3	157 7 8	40 0 4	—
Wokeing	9	8	4	30	44	62	157	37 10 10	85 17 11	12 4 6	135 13 3	49 16 9	—
Worplesdon	—	—	—	—	3	12	15	—	3 11 0	0 16 0	4 7 0	7 16 3	—
Wanborow	43	18	12	64	116	240	493	143 18 10	228 9 7	31 16 6	404 4 11	47 11 7	—
Godalming	—	—	—	15	20	45	80	—	38 3 6	3 9 8	41 13 2	5 6 10	—
Compton													
Total	88	54	60	383	560	1147	2292	347 15 5	1291 4 7	133 4 1	1772 4 1	335 1 11	80 8 1

56

Appendix 2   Guildford Union. Extract from the Quarterly Abstract for the Quarter ending 24th March 1838

GUILDFORD UNION.

EXTRACT from the QUARTERLY ABSTRACT, shewing the Number of Paupers relieved, the Amount of Money expended, and the Balances due to and from the several Parishes, for the Quarter ending the 24th of March, 1838.

PARISHES	In-door Adults Males	In-door Adults Females	In-door Children	Out-door Adults Males	Out-door Adults Females	Out-door Children	GRAND TOTAL	No. of Cases of Medical Relief Indoor	No. of Cases of Medical Relief Outdoor	Amount of Contribution to Building Workhouse £ s. d.	Proportion of In-Maintenance £ s. d.	Out-Relief £ s. d.	Proportion of Establishment Charges £ s. d.	Payments on Account of Registration Act £ s. d.	TOTAL £ s. d.	Balance due to the Parish £ s. d.	Balance due from the Parish £ s. d.
Artington	11	8	7	21	30	50	127	13	47	—	44 7 7	80 8 5	22 14 5	2 1 3	149 11 8	—	12 3 9
Guildford { Saint Nicholas	6	6	3	14	28	32	89	5	49	—	24 19 3	77 0 10	18 2 3	2 10 3	122 12 7	—	13 3 0
Guildford { Saint Mary	4	3	3	12	16	24	62	5	10	—	15 8 4	54 7 4	13 11 7	2 6 3	85 13 6	—	3 6 0
Guildford { Holy Trinity	2	3	8	20	20	5	69	10	22	—	29 12 4	63 9 9	22 0 10	1 7 9	116 10 8	16 16 0	—
Albury	8	7	4	39	47	69	174	8	39	—	27 14 10	141 4 0	32 17 7	1 10 9	203 7 2	—	4 10 1
Shere	2	1	—	6	7	19	35	1	6	—	7 0 8	16 13 8	1 18 8	1 2 9	26 15 9	—	15 2 5
East Clandon	—	—	—	11	11	21	43	—	12	—	—	33 1 10	6 2 1	0 17 9	40 1 8	—	65 10 4
West Clandon	—	1	1	5	5	13	24	—	6	—	0 10 10	15 4 5	4 3 9	1 2 9	21 1 9	4 4 6	—
East Horsley	1	1	1	15	21	76	115	3	11	—	4 8 4	63 12 8	11 14 9	1 12 9	81 8 6	—	10 9 9
West Horsley	1	1	1	6	15	29	52	1	4	—	2 0 8	31 2 2	5 6 3	1 2 3	39 11 10	—	7 10 2
Merrow	9	2	6	9	10	13	49	9	7	—	35 6 6	27 4 0	10 15 2	1 5 3	74 10 11	—	9 10 11
Ockham	6	3	4	6	13	18	50	7	3	—	25 8 10	33 12 6	10 19 8	1 1 3	71 2 3	—	4 15 2
Pirbright	8	12	12	33	44	93	202	18	26	—	63 10 11	107 9 2	34 7 6	2 5 3	207 12 10	0 5 6	—
Send and Ripley	3	1	8	30	38	66	146	6	25	294 18 2	25 9 3	119 18 6	24 14 0	1 8 3	466 8 2	—	22 2 6
Stoke	1	1	1	—	2	—	5	—	2	—	6 13 5	2 16 0	3 9 3	0 17 9	13 16 5	7 2 4	—
Wisley	13	4	11	85	75	173	361	15	96	—	55 6 7	203 2 3	40 7 8	2 12 3	301 8 9	—	56 17 1
Wokeing	16	6	13	43	53	71	202	18	25	—	69 4 5	133 5 0	37 18 9	2 3 9	242 11 11	—	13 4 5
Worplesdon	1	—	—	2	4	8	15	—	6	—	— 11	8 19 6	2 9 8	0 1 0	11 11 1	3 8 11	—
Wanboro'	35	26	37	109	136	218	561	38	135	—	191 13 8	350 9 1	98 14 10	5 5 9	646 3 4	—	47 18 9
Godalming	1	1	2	11	17	13	45	1	22	—	3 11 10	37 16 11	10 15 9	1 4 9	53 9 3	25 18 5	—
Compton																	
Total	128	87	120	477	603	1011	2426	158	553	294 18 2	632 9 2	1600 18 0	413 4 5	34 0 3	2975 10 0	57 15 8	286 4 4

57

Appendix 3   Guildford Union. Extract from the Quarterly Abstract for the Quarter ending 21st March 1840

GUILDFORD UNION.

Extract from the QUARTERLY ABSTRACT, showing the Number of Paupers relieved, the Amount of Money expended, and the Balances due to and from the several Parishes for the Quarter, ending 21st March, 1840.

PARISHES.	In-door Adults Males	In-door Adults Females	In-door Children	Out-door Adults Males	Out-door Adults Females	Out-door Children	GRAND TOTAL	No. of Cases of Medical Relief Indoor	No. of Cases of Medical Relief Outdoor	Re-payment of Workhouse Loans £ s. d.	Proportion of In-Maintenance £ s. d.	Out-Relief £ s. d.	Proportion of Establishment Charges £ s. d.	Expenses of Registration of Births, Deaths, and Marriages £ s. d.	TOTAL £ s. d.	Balance due to the Parish £ s. d.	Balance due from the Parish £ s. d.
Artington	11	4	7	28	22	58	130	9	25	11 10 8	30 17 6	87 2 6	24 18 5	0 9 6	154 18 7	—	0 14 7
Saint Nicholas } Guildford	3	3	—	19	23	51	99	2	45	10 17 3	7 9 2	91 2 4	23 9 1	1 1 6	133 19 4	1 12 8	—
Saint Mary	8	2	2	18	22	37	89	3	12	7 13 7	12 16 3	60 17 2	16 11 10	0 15 6	98 14 4	16 9 7	—
Holy Trinity	1	3	2	23	33	56	118	—	36	10 2 1	5 1 3	107 14 11	21 16 6	0 15 0	145 10 3	—	10 10 3
Albury	7	7	9	42	52	66	183	10	72	16 11 10	40 1 3	140 6 5	35 16 8	0 15 0	233 11 2	—	11 17 2
Shere	2	1	—	3	5	8	19	2	9	2 6 10	5 13 9	22 2 4	5 1 3	0 3 6	35 7 8	—	4 1 8
East Clandon	2	—	—	11	10	16	39	1	11	4 5 11	0 11 3	48 18 5	9 5 7	0 3 0	63 4 2	—	5 15 8
West Clandon	1	2	—	6	6	12	25	—	11	2 8 11	1 17 11	14 15 6	5 5 9	0 4 0	24 12 7	3 2 5	—
East Horsley	3	3	9	15	28	56	114	6	12	7 17 4	24 6 3	54 15 6	16 19 9	0 4 0	104 2 10	17 1 10	—
West Horsley	1	—	2	7	13	31	54	—	2	3 15 0	2 7 1	27 16 9	8 2 0	0 1 6	42 2 4	27 13 9	—
Merrow	7	4	10	6	13	11	51	5	9	5 17 8	30 4 7	38 10 10	12 14 3	0 8 0	87 15 4	—	9 1 10
Ockham	3	2	4	11	11	34	65	1	39	6 3 11	15 0 10	59 0 6	13 7 9	0 9 6	94 2 6	—	11 6 6
Pirbright	6	7	8	30	38	103	192	9	48	17 4 4	35 17 11	154 3 9	37 3 8	1 1 0	245 10 8	—	15 9 8
Send and Ripley	4	4	10	36	40	88	182	9	40	15 17 9	26 10 0	160 18 9	34 6 3	1 12 0	239 4 9	—	26 18 9
Stoke	—	1	2	2	3	1	9	—	3	0 17 2	1 17 11	9 4 7	1 17 1	0 1 0	13 17 9	—	1 15 5
Wisley	17	6	35	68	57	168	351	16	206	22 1 2	82 16 3	221 4 0	47 12 11	2 1 0	375 15 4	—	80 15 4
Wokeing	15	7	12	38	41	78	191	8	35	18 7 9	53 3 9	149 11 7	39 14 3	1 0 0	261 17 4	—	16 3 4
Worplesdon	—	—	—	—	3	3	6	—	9	1 3 11	—	3 11 10	2 11 9	0 2 0	7 9 6	—	—
Wanboro'	32	22	35	121	151	226	587	22	154	54 12 9	137 11 8	423 9 1	118 0 3	2 10 6	736 4 3	8 11 6	—
Godalming	2	—	—	12	18	4	36	2	16	4 13 9	2 18 4	50 7 2	10 2 6	0 8 0	68 9 9	—	5 6 9
Compton																	5 16 3
Total	125	75	146	496	589	1109	2540	113	794	224 9 7	517 2 11	1925 13 11	484 17 6	14 6 6	3166 10 5	89 1 9	205 13 2
As compared with the corresponding Quarter of last Year { Increase	7	—	16	6	—	21	41	16	—	224 9 7	—	33 11 7	72 17 6	—	248 9 1	—	—
{ Diminution	—	6	—	—	3	—	—	—	125	—	61 17 7	—	—	20 12 0	—	—	—

Appendix 4   Guildford Union. Items of Expenditure as detailed on 24th April 1840

ITEMS OF EXPENDITURE.

LOANS RE-PAID.

	£	s	d
Balance brought forward	7	14	3
Exchequer Loan Commissioners	200	0	0
Compton	20	8	8
	228	2	11
Balance carried forward	3	13	4
	224	9	7

IN-MAINTENANCE.

	£	s	d
Balance from last Quarter	226	12	9
Mr. William Chennell—Bread and Flour	107	0	8
Mr. William King—Groceries, &c.	48	10	7
Mr. F. T. Guaser—ditto	59	10	7
Messrs. Mathew and Spershott—Meat	7	15	10
Mr. Thomas White—Porter	5	3	0
Messrs. Nealds and Cooper—Wine	49	2	0
Messrs. Wilkins—Coals, &c.	0	19	8
Messrs. Bart and Copus—Buns	53	8	4
Mr. George Sylvester—Drapery	2	19	4
Mr. E. Page—Shoes	1	14	8
Mr. Daniel Woods—Leather			
Mr. Thomas Ames—Disbursements			
	577	0	1
Deduct Master's and other Officers' Provisions, 8 in number, charged to Establishment	12	3	0
Out-Relief	7	12	8
Balance carried forward	40	12	8
	£517	2	11

Average Weekly Cost per Head of the In-door Pauper.
	s	d
Food	2	7¼
Clothing	0	3
	2	11

Board Room, Guildford,
24th April, 1840.

OUT RELIEF.

	£	s	d
Cash paid by Mr. Lovett	551	10	9
Ditto by Mr. Clarke	554	5	6
Messrs. Warburton and Co. maintaining lunatic Paupers	36	11	6
Mr. H. B. Lee, ditto	37	15	6
Mr. William Chennell—Bread	303	11	4
Mr. Thomas Jacques ....ditto	134	4	7
Mr. Sherman ....ditto	80	7	7
Mr. John Thompson....ditto	68	14	3
Messrs. Mathew and Spershott—Meat	32	17	0
Mr. Charles Hart ....ditto	25	4	5
Mr. P. Daws ....ditto	12	9	3
Mr. J. Coombes ......ditto	4	18	10
Mr. James Arnold ....ditto	2	17	0
Mr. John Woods ......ditto	5	6	3
Mr. E. Bristow ....ditto	2	14	8
Mr. Bowler ....ditto	3	1	6
Mr. Lickfold ....ditto	7	0	0
Mr. Combs ....ditto	0	16	0
Mr. George Carman—Coffins	5	13	0
Mr. W. Stradwick ....ditto	2	2	0
Mr. T. Johnson ....ditto	2	12	8
Mr. James Rose ....ditto	12	8	0
Messrs. Ansell, Daborn, and Peters—Sundries	6	3	4
Mr. Stedman—Trusses	7	12	8
Mr. Parsons—ditto			
Workhouse Provisions			
	1925	13	11

ESTABLISHMENT.

	£	s	d
Balance brought forward	3	15	2
Overseers of Stoke—Poor Rate	5	10	0
Clerk .... 1 quarter's Salary	37	10	0
Auditor .... ditto	6	0	0
Chaplain .... ditto	10	0	0
Mr. Stedman, Surgeon .. ditto	15	0	0
Mr. Butler .... ditto	26	5	0
Mr. Balchin .... ditto	13	15	0
Mr. J. K. Eager ditto .. ditto	28	15	0
Mr. Davey .... ditto	32	10	0
Mr. Harbroe .... ditto	15	0	0
Mr. Lovett, Relieving Officer	10	0	0
Mr. Clark, ditto .... ditto	8	15	0
Master .... ditto	6	5	0
Matron .... ditto	2	17	9
Schoolmaster .... ditto	1	10	0
Schoolmistress ...... ditto	1	17	0
Porter .... ditto	76	18	8
Shoemaker .... ditto	7	7	3
Table .... ditto	1	4	3
Superintendent ...... ditto	3	10	0
Mess. Price and Co. Repairing Hot-air Apparatus	2	14	4
Exchequer Loan Commissioners, Interest on Loan	17	0	0
Compton .... ditto	1	13	0
Messrs. Wilkins, Carriage of Junk	8	14	8
Mr. E. Andrews, Stationery, &c.	4	4	2
Messrs. Knight and Co.—ditto	2	14	11
Mr. Baxter, Advertising	4	13	3
Mr. Lomas, Paper	9	1	0
Clerk, Disbursements	3	7	1
Mr. W. Hooks, Plumber and Glazier's Work			
Mr. Charles Cooke, Brazier's Work			
Mr. Thomas Whithorn, Furniture			
Registrar's Office—Repairing Wheelbarrows, &c.			
Mr. T. Gosling			
Thomas Smith, Shaving Paupers			
Mr. John Daborn—Funerals			
Mess. Lymposs, Charrett, Baker, Wallis, Shaw and Co. Parish Clerk of Stoke, and Many sundry small Accounts	117	5	8
Mr. Thomas Ames..Disbursements 21 1 9			
Ditto—Bones	136	7	5
Master and other Officers Rations	12	3	0
	605	10	5

Denary
	£	s	d
Mr. Newnam for Bones	33	0	0
Mr. Winkworth ...ditto	25	0	0
Mr. Daws ....ditto	20	0	0
Mr. G. Smallpeice ditto	12	0	0
Mr. E. T. Upperton ditto	3	12	0
Mr. E. Elkins .....ditto	10	0	3
Mr. W. Sparkes, Chalk	2	2	0
Mr. Phillipson.... Ditto	0	3	0
	2	15	8
Balance carried forward	121	1	11
	484	17	6

REGISTRATION.

	£	s	d
Mr. Richard Eager, Registrar of the Guildford District, for Fees	3	18	6
Mr. Richard Balchin, Registrar of the Godalming District, for Fees	3	0	0
Mr. John Hooper, Registrar of the Woking District, for Fees	3	10	0
Mr. John Higgins, Registrar of the Shere District, for Fees	2	7	0
Mr. Henry White, Registrar of the Ripley District, for Fees	1	10	0
	14	6	6

TOTALS.

	£	s	d
Loans re-paid	224	9	7
In-maintenance	517	2	11
Out-Relief	1925	13	11
Establishment	484	17	6
Registration	14	6	6
	£3166	10	5

George S. Smallpeice,
Clerk to the Board of Guardians.

Russells' Printers.

Appendix 5   Abstract of the Census of the Population of the Guildford District of the Guildford Union, taken 7th June 1841

Abstract of the Census of the Population of the Guildford District of the Guildford Union, taken the 7th June, 1841.

G. W. BAILEY, H. V. LOMAS.	ENUMERATORS' NAMES. J. JENNER, C. PIGGOTT.	J. ELLIS, A. THAYRE.	W. STURT, P. BLAKE.				
DESCRIPTION	Uninhabited Houses.	Houses Building.	Inhabited Houses	Males.	Females.	Totals.	COMBINED Uninhabited Houses.	Houses Building.	PAROCHIAL Inhabited Houses	TOTALS. Males.	Females.	Total Population.

DESCRIPTION	Uninhab. Houses	Houses Building	Inhab. Houses	Males	Females	Totals	Comb. Uninhab. Houses	Houses Building	Paroch. Inhab. Houses	Males	Females	Total Pop.
SAINT MARY'S PARISH.												
1. All that part of the parish of Saint Mary's, Guildford, as is situate on the South side of High Street, from No. 124, High Street, to the East corner of Quarry Street, with Quarry Street, Chapel Street, Castle Street, Mill Lane, and the Lanes and Alleys, &c., to the South of High Street.	10	0	145	427	464	891						
2. All that part of the parish of Saint Mary's, Guildford, as is situate in the High Street, from the West corner of Quarry Street, to the river Wey, the North side of High Street, from the river Wey to No. 47, High Street, with Friary Street, Friary Place, Swan Lane, Angel Gate, Alexander's Row, North Street, and the Courts and Alleys North of High Street.	11	0	131	360	425	785	21	0	276	787	889	1676
HOLY TRINITY PARISH.												
3. All that part of the parish of Holy Trinity, Guildford, as is situate on the South side of High Street, commencing at No. 125, and ending at No. 144, both numbers included. Trinity Church Yard, Smithy Street, Milkhouse Gate, Tuns Gate, Loop Gate, Smallpeice's Gate, and such other parts of the above Parish as are situate South of High Street, excluding the House of Correction.	7	0	121	302	341	643						
4. All that part of the Parish of Holy Trinity, Guildford, as is situate on the North side of High Street from Richardson's, No. 145 to 162, both inclusive, with Ellis's Passage, Whitburn's Gate, Rat's Castle, Poyle Cottage, Potter's, North side of High Street, from No. 1 to No. 46, both inclusive, Fourth Building, Star's Buildings, North Street, Market Street, and Whitburn's Gate, with all other Courts and Alleys, North of High Street, exclusive of Abbott's Hospital and the Royal Grammar School.	4	0	111	314	342	656	11	0	232	616	683	1299
SAINT NICHOLAS PARISH.												
5. All that part of the Parish of Saint Nicholas, Guildford, situate in, and known by the name of the Tything of Artington.	3	0	126	321	336	657						
6. All that part of the Parish of Saint Nicholas not situate within the Tything of Artington.	12	4	154	433	459	892	15	4	280	754	825	1579
STOKE PARISH.												
7. All that part of the Parish of Stoke, comprised in Spital Street, School House Lane, such parts as are situate in and South East of the road leading from Guildford to London, Stoke Park, Stoke Mills, Stoke Lock, and such parts of the Parish of Stoke as are situate beyond the river Wey, exclusive of the Union Workhouse.	9	1	146	362	399	761						
8. All that part of the Parish of Stoke having for its boundaries the road leading from Guildford to Woodbridge on the West, Joseph's Lane on the North, and Stoke Lane, with the road leading from Stoke Lane to Stoke Bridge on the East, including the Lees, Dapdune, Stoke Parsonage, and Stoke Lane, but excluding the Leu Pale house Lunatic Asylum.	18	4	217	481	586	1067	27	5	363	843	985	1828
Guildford House of Correction				102	28	130						
Archbishop Abbott's Hospital				13	9	22						
Royal Grammar School				48	5	53						
Guildford Union Workhouse				108	109	217						
Leu Pale house Lunatic Asylum				5	4	9						
							74	9	1151	3276	3537	6813
									431			

[Printed and Sold by G. W. & J. Russell.]

Appendix 6 Guildford Union. Extract from the Quarterly Abstract for the Quarter ending 21st September 1844

GUILDFORD UNION.

Extract from the QUARTERLY ABSTRACT, shewing the Number of Paupers Relieved, the Amount of Money Expended, and the Balances due to and from the several Parishes, for the Quarter ending the 21st of September, 1844.

Population in 1841.	PARISHES.	IN-DOOR Males.	IN-DOOR Females.	IN-DOOR Children.	OUT-DOOR Males.	OUT-DOOR Females.	OUT-DOOR Children.	GRAND TOTAL.	No. of Cases of Medical Relief. In-door	Outdoor	Repayment of Workhouse Loans. £ s d	Proportion of In-maintenance. £ s d	Out Relief. £ s d	Proportion of Establishment Charges. £ s d	Total Expenditure for the Relief of the Poor. £ s d	Registration Fees. £ s d	Vaccination Fees. £ s d	Total Expenditure including Relief to the Poor, Registration, and Vaccination Fees. £ s d	Balance due to the Parish. £ s d	Balance due from the Parish. £ s d
1579	Artington	8	4	6	33	41	66	158	4	37	33 15 0	24 12 9	97 17 0	20 12 6	176 17 3	0 14 6	0 7 6	177 19 3	10 14 5	—
1676	Saint Nicholas	17	4	9	28	44	65	167	14	41	33 18 0	26 18 6	98 16 11	20 14 4	180 7 7	1 0 0	1 2 6	182 10 1	6 19 3	—
1606	Saint Mary	5	2	4	14	32	43	96	3	18	21 12 0	7 11 10	65 9 0	13 4 0	107 17 0	1 0 0	0 10 0	109 7 0	11 7 8	—
1079	Holy Trinity	1	—	—	35	44	105	189	—	29	33 1 6	7 3 7	101 0 0	20 4 8	161 9 10	0 5 0	0 5 4	162 5 4	22 12 4	—
1347	Albury	5	3	5	67	79	135	294	8	52	51 5 0	16 14 6	173 8 10	31 7 0	272 16 4	0 10 0	1 2 6	274 8 10	12 7 2	—
293	Shere	—	—	—	4	9	—	16	—	6	5 5 0	—	21 7 5	9 1 6	34 13 3	0 7 9	—	34 14 9	35 10 8	—
407	East Clandon	1	—	—	9	11	25	41	—	11	14 17 0	1 14 1	21 14 4	9 1 6	47 6 1	0 14 3	—	47 10 3	8 2 5	—
300	West Clandon	2	—	—	9	18	29	48	1	8	5 15 6	1 19 0	18 12 4	4 3 10	29 18 2	0 1 5	—	29 19 8	13 4 8	—
671	East Horsley	—	—	3	19	33	70	125	2	22	22 11 6	5 2 4	70 19 0	13 15 11	112 9 8	0 10 0	—	112 19 8	13 10 6	—
252	West Horsley	—	4	—	10	15	14	48	3	14	11 12 6	3 11 7	36 12 4	7 2 1	58 18 6	0 7 0	—	59 7 6	5 10 6	—
640	Merrow	3	3	8	22	26	42	104	8	16	16 16 0	17 12 10	70 7 6	11 10 1	118 13 11	—	—	118 13 11	20 2 10	13 9 3
657	Ockham	1	3	3	21	20	50	97	2	13	21 12 0	9 18 0	53 4 6	13 4 0	97 18 4	0 10 0	2 7 6	100 11 10	37 14 8	—
1538	Pirbright	2	—	6	46	64	92	213	10	31	54 12 0	15 7 10	163 3 6	33 6 3	266 10 0	0 19 0	0 15 0	267 9 0	61 16 4	—
2054	Send and Ripley	6	5	15	35	59	110	230	3	62	56 5 0	30 18 10	129 4 2	34 7 6	250 14 8	1 3 0	—	252 12 6	—	—
155	Stoke	2	1	—	8	14	33	33	1	4	4 4 4	9 18 0	15 17 2	2 9 6	24 9 0	8 1	1 7 0	24 11 2	35 16 2	—
2482	Wokeing	11	10	28	61	83	169	362	22	94	80 18 6	59 15 6	223 3 8	49 9 1	413 6 7	2 17 6	0 10 0	416 11 1	22 19 7	—
1424	Worplesdon	17	9	10	46	64	76	222	16	44	56 14 0	41 12 0	159 19 7	34 13 0	292 8 7	1 6 0	—	294 0 0	3 16 6	—
171	Wanborough	—	—	—	2	2	2	6	—	2	2 14 0	2 16 3	6 15 9	1 4 6	11 2 9	1 5 9	—	11 5 6	80 18 9	1 18 8
4328	Godalming	27	15	25	143	185	262	667	33	150	168 10 0	82 7 4	478 3 1	102 19 9	832 0 11	2 13 6	17 7 6	852 1 11	7 1 0	—
522	Compton	1	—	—	14	19	15	25	1	—	14 14 0	2 1 5	49 18 11	8 19 8	73 13 0	0 3 0	—	74 6 0	—	—
	Total	108	73	120	626	842	1400	3169	137	663	715 11 6	355 7 1	2055 1 6	437 5 11	3563 13 0	13 11 6	26 10 0	3603 7 10	412 0 1	15 7 11
23,081	Increase	8	—	1	92	65	88	217	54	1	9 18 11	1 12 3	184 8 7	129 4 1	63 11 2	0 2 0	18 0 0	45 13 2	—	—
	Diminution	—	9	27																

ITEMS OF EXPENDITURE.

LOANS RE-PAID.

	£ s d
Balance brought forward	9 5 8
Exchequer Loan Commissioners	30 0 0
Wm. Hayden, Esq.	35 14 0
Saint Nicholas	22 15 0
Saint Mary	46 0 0
Holy Trinity	45 0 0
Albury	42 10 0
Shere	30 8 0
East Clandon	14 0 0
West Horsley	25 3 0
Merrow	15 0 0
Ockham	46 10 0
Stoke	20 0 0
Wisley	10 1 0

OUT RELIEF.

	£ s d
Cash paid by Mr. Bender	659 0 4
Ditto, by Mr. Clark	563 0 0
The Trustees of the Surrey County Lunatic Asylum, maintaining Lunatic Paupers	70 2 4
Mr. Wm. Chennell .... Bread	103 1 3
Mrs. Wick .... ditto	143 2 5
Mr. Sherman .... ditto	108 0 0
Mr. Thompson .... ditto	15 0 0
Mr. Gwinn .... ditto	39 9 0
Mr. Parson ...... Midwifery, Surgical Cases, &c.	19 15 0
Mr. Davey .... ditto	11 8 0
Mr. Butler .... ditto	6 3 0

ESTABLISHMENT.

	£ s d
Balance brought forward	10 8 9
Interest on Exchequer Loans	56 11 10
Ditto on Parish Loans	68 11 0
Ditto to Wm. Hayden, Esq.	2 16 6
Overseers of Stoke—Poor Rate	37 10 0
Clerk .... One Quarter's Salary	6 5 0
Auditor .... ditto	15 0 0
Chaplain .... ditto	10 0 0
Mr. Stedman—Surgeon	18 15 0
Mr. Butler—Ditto	21 5 0
Mr. Parson—Ditto	11 5 0
Mr. J. K. Eager—Ditto	—
Mr. Davey—Ditto	—

REGISTRATION.

	£ s d
Mr. Richard Eager, Registrar of the Guildford District, for Fees	3 18 0
Mr. Richard Balchin, Registrar of the Godalming District, for Fees	2 19 6
Mr. W. Rose, Registrar of the Woking District, for Fees	3 5 0
Mr. John Higgins, Registrar of the Albury District, for Fees	2 1 0
Mr. Henry White, Registrar of the Ripley District, for Fees	1 8 0

Appendix 7 — Items of Expenditure as detailed on 23rd October 1844

	£	s	d
Balance brought forward	9	8	0
Exchequer Loan Commissioners	300	0	0
Wm. Haydon, Esq.	35	0	0
Saint Nicholas	22	15	0
Saint Mary	46	5	0
Holy Trinity	46	18	0
Albury	42	10	0
Shere	30	8	0
East Clandon	14	0	0
West Horsley	28	0	0
Merrow	3	3	0
Ockham	40	10	0
Stoke	29	9	0
Wisley	10	7	0
Woking	35	7	0
Balance carried forward	716	2	8
	0	11	6
	£715	**11**	**6**

IN-MAINTENANCE.

	£	s	d
Balance from last quarter	14	9	7
Mr. Henry Moline ......Flour	29	5	0
Mr. Wm. Chennell ......Bread	119	9	0
Mr. John Matthew ......Meat	41	11	3
Mr. John Pannell ......Cheese 31 4 0			
Pork 18 7 0			
Sundries 21 7 7	71	0	7
Mr. Charles Foster ...Groceries	12	2	8
Mr. Chitman ......Tea, &c.	10	13	6
Messrs. Rendle and Co. ...Wine	4	0	0
Mr. Jesse Boxall ......Porter	1	4	0
Mr. Thomas White ......Gin	1	10	0
Mr. Wm. Mills ......Potatoes	29	10	0
Mr. Bridger ......Coals	35	11	1
Mr. George Silvester ......Drapery, &c.	6	11	5
Mr. Morris ......Leather	11	1	7
Mr. Ames ......Sundries	393	17	1
Deduct Officers' Provisions charged to Establishment	10	19	4
Out Relief	11	13	5
Balance carried forward	15	17	3
	£355	**7**	**1**

AVERAGE WEEKLY COST PER HEAD OF THE IN-DOOR PAUPERS.

	s	d
Food	2	4
Clothing	0	3½
	2	7½

BOARD ROOM, GUILDFORD,
23rd October, 1844.

	£	s	d
Balance brought forward	680	0	4
Interest on Exchequer Loans	563	0	0
Ditto on Parish Loans	70	2	4
Ditto to Wm. Haydon, Esq.			
Overseers of Stoke—Poor Rate	108	2	0
Clerk, } One Quarter's Salary	143	0	0
Chaplain ......ditto	73	0	0
Auditor ......ditto	55	15	1
Mr. Stedman—Surgeon ......ditto	39	9	0
Mr. Butler ......Ditto ......ditto	10	15	2
Mr. Parsons—Midwifery, Surgical Cases, &c. ......ditto	11	8	0
Mr. Davey ......Ditto ......ditto	13	5	0
Mr. Sells ......Ditto ......ditto	5	3	0
Mr. Gall ......Ditto ......ditto	0	15	0
Mr. Stedman ......ditto	4	14	0
Mr. Fletcher—Ditto ......ditto	3	5	0
Mr. Brasier—Relieving Officer ......ditto	32	10	0
Mr. Clark ......ditto ......ditto	32	10	0
Master ......ditto	17	10	0
Matron ......ditto	12	10	0
Schoolmaster ......ditto	8	15	0
Schoolmistress ......ditto	6	5	0
Porter ......ditto, &c.	6	5	0
Messrs. Williams and Filmer—Ironmonger	7	5	11
Messrs. Randall and Son—Plumber	18	2	7
Messrs. Knight and Co.—Stationery	2	14	8
Clerk's Disbursements	4	6	1
Mr. E. Andrews—Printing, &c.	6	8	0
Rent—Register Office	3	15	0
Mrs. Wallis—Cooper	4	11	3
Mr. Quelch—Straw	6	3	0
Mr. Durnford—Funerals	5	13	11
Messrs. Baxter, Lee, Fabers, Dickinson, Moseley, and Heyman ......Sundries	3	12	11
Messrs. Pannell, White, and Mills ......ditto			
Mr. Thomas Ames—Bones 68 0 7			
Wages 14 19 9			
Sundries 8 2 1	91	2	5
Officers' Rations	10	10	4
	£590	**18**	**10**

Cash paid by Mr. Brasier
Ditto by Mr. Clark
The Trustees of the Surrey County Lunatic Asylum, maintaining Lunatic Paupers

Mr. Wm. Chennell ......Bread			
Mrs. Wick ......ditto			
Mr. Sherman ......ditto			
Mr. Thompson ......ditto			
Mr. Gwinn ......ditto			
Mr. Parson—Coats ......ditto			
Mr. Davey ......ditto			
Mr. Butler ......ditto			
Mr. Sells ......ditto			
Mr. Stedman ......ditto			
Mr. Gall ......ditto			
Mr. Fletcher ......ditto			
Messrs. Hart and Son ......ditto			
Mr. P. Daws ......ditto			
Mr. John Matthew ......ditto			
Mr. Gregory ......ditto, &c.			
Mr. Coniabee ......ditto			
Mr. Bristow ......ditto			
Mr. Clark ......ditto			
Mr. Arnold ......ditto			
Mr. J. Coombes ......ditto			
Mr. Richards ......ditto			
Mr. John May ......ditto			
Mr. John Woods ......ditto			
Mr. H. Bristow ......ditto			
Mr. Widdows ......ditto			
Mr. George Silvester ......Groceries, &c.			
Messrs. Reading and Jaques ......ditto			
Mr. Pannell ......ditto			
Messrs. Boxall and White ......Porter			
Mr. Silvester ......Drapery, &c.			
Mr. Rideridger ......Porter			
Mrs. E. Hooper ......ditto			
Mr. R. Richards ......ditto			
Messrs. White, Langrish, and Peters ......ditto			
Messrs. Pullen, Freeland, Woods & Page, Clothes			
Messrs. Westbrooks, Mills and Killick—Beaumont, Smith, Rogers, Underwood, and Sundries			
Messrs. Furhall, Collier, Richbell, Beaumont, Sundries	7	1	0
Messrs. Miles, Linegar, Child, & Smith—Coffins	3	9	6
Mr. Ford ......ditto	9	7	0
Mr. Curnan ......ditto	8	5	0
Mr. Heynes ......ditto	5	0	0
Mr. Strudwick ......ditto	10	10	6
Mr. W. Bye ......ditto	2	2	0
Workhouse—Wine and Provisions	11	13	5
	£2055	**1**	**10**

Mr. Richard Eager, Registrar of the Guildford District, for Fees	3	18	0
Mr. Richard Dalchin, Registrar of the Godalming District, for Fees	2	19	6
Mr. W. Ross, Registrar of the Woking District, for Fees	3	5	0
Mr. John Higgins, Registrar of the Albury District, for Fees	2	1	0
Mr. Henry White, Registrar of the Ripley District, for Fees	1	8	0
	£13	**11**	**6**

VACCINATION.

	£	s	d
Mr. James Stedman, Surgeon, Guildford	0	7	6
Mr. W. H. Butler, ditto, dito	3	0	0
Mr. C. A. Parson, ditto, Godalming	17	15	6
Mr. T. J. Sells, ditto, Guildford	2	17	6
Mr. Fletcher, ditto, Woking	1	7	6
Mr. Davey, ditto, Shere	1	2	6
	£26	**10**	**0**

TOTALS.

	£	s	d
Loans re-paid	715	11	6
In-maintenance	355	7	1
Out Relief	2055	1	10
Establishment	437	5	11
Registration	13	11	6
Vaccination	26	10	0
	£3603	**7**	**10**

Mr. John Sparkes ......Bone dust	36	0	0
Mr. R. Sparkes ......ditto	27	0	0
Capt. Wight ......ditto	25	4	0
Messrs. G., F., and J. Smallpeice ......ditto	12	12	0
Mr. H. Moline ......ditto	10	16	0
Mr. Geo. Smallpeice ......ditto	9	15	9
Mr. Elkins ......ditto	6	5	0
Mr. Churchman ......ditto	4	10	0
Mr. D. Hooker ......ditto	4	10	0
Mr. Baxter ......ditto	2	5	0
Mr. Bennett ......ditto	2	7	6
Rev. A. Onslow ......ditto	0	15	0
Mr. H. Smallpeice—Carding Flocks	1	10	6
Balance	8	6	2
	163	12	11
	£437	**5**	**11**

W. HAYDON SMALLPEICE,
Clerk to the Board of Guardians.

[RUSSELLS, PRINTERS, GUILDFORD.]

Afterword

At the time of completing this booklet in August 2003, the Vagrants' Casual Ward is still owned by the developers, Crest Nicholson Ltd. However, it is hoped that a future use for the building will soon be found that will make it an asset for Guildford, allowing public access and bringing new life to the Vagrants' Casual Ward in the twenty first century.

Sources

Davies, Paul M. *The South West Surrey Hospitals 1859-1991. A Short Outline of their Origins and Development.* 1993. South West Surrey Health Authority.

Green, J.K. *Sidelights on Guildford History II.* 1953.
Sidelights on Guildford History III. 1954.
Sidelights on Guildford History IV. 1956.
Reprinted edition by permission of the Surrey Times.

Gould, J. *Old Merrow.* 1948. Facsimile Edition. 1988. Peter Knee.

Harris, Jose. *Private Lives Public Spirit. A Social History of Britain 1870-1914.* 1993. Oxford University Press.

Harrison, J.F.C. *Late Victorian Britain 1875-1901.* 1990. Fontana Press.

Inglesant, George David. *The early years of the Guildford Poor Law Union 1834-1838.* 1980. References included from *A history of the Poor Law and of the parishes which formed the Guildford Poor Law Union, leading to the passing of the Poor Law Amendment Act of 1834 and until the formation of the Poor Law Board of 1847.* Hazel R. Jones. 1958. Surrey Archaeological Society Library.

Ives, A.G.L. *British Hospitals.* MCMXLVIII. Collins, London.

Johnson, Paul.   *A Place in History.*
                          1974. Weidenfeld & Nicholson.

May, Trevor.   *The Victorian Workhouse.*
                          1997. Shire Publications Ltd.

Morrison, Kathryn.   *The Workhouse. A Study of Poor Law Buildings in England.*
                          1999. English Heritage.

Noyes, Ann.   *Shere Poverty. From Parish Workhouse to Union Workhouse.*
                          1996. Twiga Books, Gomshall, Surrey.

Reid, Andy.   *The Union Workhouse. A study guide for local historians and teachers.*
                          1994. Phillimore for British Association for Local History.

Stemp, David.   *Three Acres & A Cow. The life and works of Eli Hamshire.*
                          1995.

Taylor, Brian.   *Abbot's Hospital Guildford.*
                          1999. St Thomas's Trust, Guildford.

Thompson, Beryl.   *Life in the Workhouse, Booklet 3, Vagrants.*
                          1996. Ripon Museum Trust.

Wheeleker, Susannah   *Poor Relief in Devon.*
& Eyles, Sarah.   1991. The Devonshire Association.

Further source material:

'*Living London*'. First published 1902 by Cassell & Co Ltd.
Reprinted as '*Edwardian London*'. 1990. The Village Press Ltd. '

Sources relating to the Guildford Union Workhouse and Vagrants' Casual Ward.
Reproduced by permission of Surrey History Service.
Copyright of Surrey History Service:

BG6/11/29, 30, 31, 32, 33, 34, 35. Minutes of the Board of Guardians
BG6/12/2. Minutes of the Finance Committee.
BG6/12/7,8,9. Minutes of the House (later Visiting) Committee.
BG6/80/1. Instructions to set up the Guildford Poor Law Union.
CC767/22/8/1. South East Counties Joint Vagrancy Committee.

Bibliography of other suggested useful reference sources

Mike Brown. Published by Dartmoor Press Guides for Family and Local History Researchers. Dartmoor Press, PO Box 132, Plymouth PL4 7YL:

Vol.14 Transcripts of Acts and Statutes: Vol.2. 1601 Poor Relief Act
Vol.15 Transcripts of Acts and Statutes: Vol.3. 1662 Act of Settlement
Vol.16 Transcripts of Acts and Statutes: Vol.4. 1722 Workhouse Act
Vol.10 Transcripts of Acts and Statutes: Vol.1. 1834 Poor Law Amendment Act

Poor Law Union Records.
Published by The Federation of Family History Societies, 2-4 Killer Street, Ramsbottom, Bury, Lancashire BL0 9BZ:

Part 1. South-East England and East Anglia
Part 2. The Midlands and Northern England
Part 3. South-West England, The Marches and Wales
Part 4. Gazetteer of England and Wales

Glossary of Terms

The hundred. The smaller unit into which counties were divided, which had appeared as units of local government in the tenth century.

Casual. A term referring to a vagrant or tramp, or to someone on the road in search of work.

Ward. A separate room or division in a hospital, etc.

Casual ward or vagrants' casual ward. A building associated with a workhouse containing cells to accommodate vagrants or tramps.

Cell. A small single-occupancy sleeping room, sometimes with attached work room, in a vagrants' casual ward, into which the casuals were locked and bolted at night.

Indoor relief. The provision of shelter in a workhouse.

Outdoor relief. The provision of short-term relief in the form of money, food, fuel or rent financed from the poor rate.

Paupers. Those in destitute circumstances with no form of income.

Inmates. The term used to describe the pauper occupants of the workhouse, an institution designed to resemble a prison.

Able-bodied pauper or poor. Adults under the age of 60 capable of working but unable to find employment.

Impotent pauper or poor. Those incapable of work, e.g. the elderly, infirm, mentally ill or permanently sick and infants.

A manufactory. An early term for a small factory or place of work set up particularly to provide work for paupers.

Oakum. From an old English word meaning "off combings".

To pick oakum. The picking apart of used hemp or jute ropes with the aid of a spike to provide fibres for caulking ships.

The spike, the bastille, the house. Names by which the workhouse and vagrants' casual ward were known. Spikes were used in oakum-picking, a hated task given to inmates; bastille after the famous prison in Paris.

Union Lane or Union Road. Usually an indication of the site of a former workhouse.